*This Book
Is Presented
To*

_____

*By*

_____

*On This Day*

_____

# Sing A New Song

## Inspirations from the Heart

# Sing A New Song

*Inspirations from the Heart*

Compiled by Mary Beckwith

**Evergreen Publications, Inc.**
Kingsley, Michigan

*SING A NEW SONG*
*Inspirations From the Heart*

*Published by:*
*Evergreen Publications, Inc.*
*8619 M-37 S.*
*Kingsley, Michigan 49649*

*Scripture quotations in this publication are taken from:*

AMP—From *The Amplified Bible*. Old Testament copyright © 1965,1987 by The Zondervan Corporation. The Amplified New Testament copyright © 1958,1987 by The Lockman Foundation. Used by permission.

JB—*Jerusalem Bible*, © 1966 by Darton, Longman and Todd, Ltd. and Doubleday and Co., Inc.

KJV—*King James Version*. Public domain.

NASB—Scripture taken from the *New American Standard Bible*, © 1960,1962,1963,1968,1971,1972,1973,1975,1977 by The Lockman Foundation. Used by permission.

NIV—From the *Holy Bible, New International Version*. Copyright © 1973,1978,1984 International Bible Society. Used by permission of Zondervan Bible Publishers.

NKJV—From the *New King James Version*. Copyright © 1979, 1980,1982, Thomas Nelson Inc., Publishers. Used by permission.

RSV—From *Revised Standard Version* of the Bible, copyrighted 1946 and 1952 by the Division of Christian Education of the NCCC, U.S.A.

TLB—Scripture verses are taken from *The Living Bible* © 1971 owned by assignment by Illinois Regional Bank N.A. (as trustee). Used by permission of Tyndale House Publishers, Inc., Wheaton, IL 60189. All rights reserved.

Library of Congress Catalog Card Number 91-38069

97 96 95 94 93 92 91    9 8 7 6 5 4 3 2 1
Printed in the United States of America

*Sing A New Song*
*is*
*dedicated*
*to*
*Paula,*
*my sweet sister*
*and dear friend.*
*Thank you*
*for all the ways*
*you say*
*I love you!*

# Contents

# Sing A New Song

**Mary Beckwith**

*He put a new song in my heart, a*
*hymn of praise to our God.*
Psalm 40:3, *NIV*

I know I'm not the first to be a
new grandmother. But, oh, the joy that entered my
life just a little over a year and a half ago. On
February 5, 1990, Daniel Jordan was born to my
daughter Laura and son-in-law Russ. I remember
telling Laura shortly after Danny's birth, "I think
I've fallen in love all over again!"

I fairly make a fool of myself now at the slightest
little thing he says or does. You'd think we were the
only grandmother and grandson in the world!

Of course, I'd heard other grandmothers share
their stories, but until I could experience
grandmothering for myself I never truly understood
or appreciated how they felt.

I met a new mom a few months ago. She was in
her mid-thirties and just starting her family. She
told me that she had never wanted children for the
first several years of her marriage. During that time
her friends and associates would go on about their
children and tell her how great it was being a
parent, but because she had never experienced it for
herself, she couldn't understand and appreciate how
her friends felt.

Then she had her child; her life changed completely and she experienced a fulfillment like never before. "I can't imagine life without my son," she shared.

My own experience as a grandmother and that of the new mom remind me of our relationship with Christ. Before we meet Him, we hear others talk about Jesus, about the way He changes lives and the joy they now feel becausing of knowing Him. But until we experience that relationship for ourselves, we can't truly understand and appreciate how they feel.

I'm so thankful to be a grandmother. It is truly a gift from the Lord. And I'm thankful for the love that that young mom feels for her child. But more than that, I'm thankful that God chose to reveal His Son Jesus Christ to me in such a personal way on that special day in May of 1984. Since then my life has not been the same; I know joy that's indescribable, and if I go on about all that He says to me from His word and all the things He does in my life, then I'm grateful for the opportunity to sing His praises.

My prayer, dear reader, is that you will find within the pages of this book fresh glimpses of the One who wants to be part of your life, Who wants to give you joy and fulfillment like never before, Who wants to put a new song in your heart.

*Dear God, I sing a hymn of praise to You. Amen.*

Mary Beckwith has compiled *Songs From the Heart, Still Moments*, and co-compiled *A Moment A Day* and *Time Out! A Men's Devotional*. She is publisher of Evergreen Publications, the mother of three, and grandmother of one. Mary and her husband, Clint, make their home in Kingsley, Michigan.

# One Special Balloon

**Niki Anderson**

*The eyes of the Lord are upon the
righteous, and his ears are open unto
their cry.* Psalm 34:15, *KJV*

At the count of three, let go of
your balloon," instructed the Sunday School teacher.
Jodie, my seven-year-old, stood poised for the
moment, clutching her blue balloon. A crowd of
parents and seventy-five children had gathered in
the church parking lot to release helium balloons
containing invitations to Sunday School.

"One, two, three!" came the shout. Instantly, a
rainbow of balloons wafted upward.

Looking skyward, Jodie pointed to the distant
cluster of colored dots. "Look, Mommy, look! There's
mine! Do you see it?"

"Of course I do," I fibbed.

A friend and I exchanged smiles of amusement.
How could Jodie know which balloon was hers? The
breeze had blown them in dances of movement for
many blocks away. My adult mind was thinking,

*With their similar shapes and duplicate colors, dear Jodie, you surely don't know which balloon is yours!*

But she *was* sure. "Watch my balloon, Mommy. There it goes!"

Jodie and her balloon are much like God and His children. When I think about the millions of people on earth, I marvel that each one is distinctive to God. How incredulous that we are never lost among the masses.

As surely as Jodie knew the specific location of her blue balloon, God knows where I am geographically, emotionally, and spiritually. Though at times I may feel blown away and aimless, He is watching me. Perhaps He looks down from heaven and says to the angels, "Look! Do you see? That child is mine!"

*Dear Father, I am thankful for Your watchful care— Your eyes are always upon me. I will take courage in knowing I can never escape Your careful gaze. Amen.*

Niki Anderson has written several articles and dozens of devotionals. She teaches writing classes through her community college and enjoys exercising, home decorating, and being involved in her children's activities. Niki and her husband have a son and a daughter and make their home in Spokane, Washington.

# Sing Thoughtful Praises

**Marlene Bagnull**

*Sing out your praises to our God, our
King. Yes, sing your highest praises to
our King, the King of all the earth.
Sing thoughtful praises!*
Psalm 47:6-7, *TLB*

It was a spur of the moment "let's
get away from everything" mini-vacation. Our
married daughter assured us that it was no problem
to come and watch our two school-age children. She
almost pushed us out the door!

During the three-hour drive to the state park
cabin, my mind replayed the nonstop problems of the
past months—my mother's illness, time pressures,
job stress. *We really do need to get away*, I told
myself. But trudging through the snow to our cabin
door, I began to question the wisdom of our decision.

"Look, someone left wood for a fire," my husband,
Paul, said. Soon a roaring fire blazed. Moments later
dense smoke filled the cabin, choking us.

"Some getaway," I grumbled. We flung open the
windows, and the cold night air poured in. Finally
we got the fireplace working and the cabin relatively

smoke free. Exhausted and still shivering, I crawled inside my sleeping bag, coat and all. I slept fitfully, exchanging my worry about problems at home for worry about the fireplace.

The morning dawned crisp and clear. The sun glistening on the ice and snow almost blinded me. I breathed in the clean, fresh air and said my first "Thank You, Lord" prayer in weeks.

Hand in hand, Paul and I went exploring after breakfast. We shed our coats as the sun grew hot. Enormous chunks of ice broke free and floated down the river. Paul spotted some fish and rushed off for his pole.

Again I began to grumble until I suddenly remembered my last minute decision to bring my autoharp. I retrieved it from the car and set it down on a dry rock downstream from Paul. As I lifted it from the case, I felt sad. It had been months since I'd played it. Amazingly it was still in tune.

I began to play and sing my favorite worship songs. My worry about problems at home lifted as I concentrated on the words and began to praise God for who He is and all He has done in my life. His presence was very real. Yes, I had needed to get away. I had needed to get away and be alone with the Lord.

*Help me, Lord, to make time daily to sing thoughtful praises. Amen.*

Marlene Bagnull is the founder of the Greater Philadelphia Christian Writers' Fellowship and director of their yearly conference. She is the author of three books and numerous articles, devotions, and poems. She and her husband, Paul, have three children and reside in Drexel Hill, Pennsylvania.

# The Beauty of Death

**Esther M. Bailey**

*Precious in the sight of the LORD is
the death of his saints.*
Psalm 116:15, *KJV*

**W**hen I returned to the office
from an out-of-town visit, a message on my desk
prompted an immediate trip to the funeral home.
The wife of the accountant for the company where I
worked had died suddenly. I had never met her, but
Irv had always spoken highly of his wife.

I expected Irv to be distraught when I arrived at
the funeral home, but he was well composed. His
spirits were upbeat as he led me to the casket to
introduce me to his wife, almost as though she were
alive. Even in death, she seemed to portray the
qualities so admired by her husband.

The funeral arrangements were of prime concern
to Irv. From his wife's Bible, which would go to the
grave with her, he had taken a poem that described
her love for God's Word. He would read it at the
funeral.

It was exciting to Irv to learn that his wife had spoken to a lady in the choir on the Sunday preceding her death. After expressing appreciation for the choir number, she had said, "I'd like to have that song sung at my funeral."

"I want the service to make a lasting impression on the grandchildren," Irv said. He prayed they would catch the faith of their grandmother.

As I left the funeral home, I understood for the first time that death can be beautiful. When my own mother died a few years later, I was able to think of the positive aspects of her passing from this life. Not only was she free from her suffering, she was going to something far better than anything she had ever experienced.

Of course death brings sorrow to those who are left behind. A sense of personal loss is bound to follow. The hope of being reunited, though, provides a note of victory that transcends tragedy.

About a month after his wife's death, Irv said, "I don't worry about her because I know where she is. But I miss her very much." The beauty of death was still present even in his time of mourning.

*Dear Lord, help me to live the kind of life that will assure those who grieve my death that I have gone to be with You. May my life also serve as an invitation to others to join me in heaven. Amen.*

Esther M. Bailey has written numerous articles, stories, and programs. In addition to writing she enjoys needlework and sewing. Esther has one grown son and currently makes her home with her husband in Phoenix, Arizona.

# The Old Toolbox

**Audrey Barcus**

*Even in old age they will produce
fruit and be vital and green.*
Psalm 92:14, *TLB*

Old age didn't faze my father one
bit. He kept fit and active, his step as sprightly as
always. Even after he retired as a carpenter, he built
a beautiful house for my mother and himself.

He became the neighborhood handyman in their
quiet New Jersey community. To my mother's
dismay, he was in constant demand to repair or
build something for his neighbors. And he never said
no. Off he'd go with his toolbox, a wink, and a smile.

Anything broken—from a doll to a lamp—he'd
mend for friends and family. We all lovingly dubbed
him Mr. Fix-it. In his spare time, he crafted
treasured doll dressers for his granddaughters and
weather vanes for his grandsons. On rainy days we'd
find him puttering by his workbench in the
basement.

He'd work on high ladders and sloping roofs that

no one else would dare climb. We still chuckle about the day he was stranded on my brother's roof for many hours when the wind knocked his ladder to the ground and no one was home.

Although his hands were always busy, my father was a quiet man, content to listen to conversations, to read his newspaper and Bible. But he spoke when it mattered. While he was in his mid-eighties, his church built an addition to their sanctuary, relying on volunteer labor from the congregation. No one was more faithful than my father. He'd pick up his toolbox and work all day at his beloved church.

My father died at ninety-one. At his funeral, a lady I'd never met approached me with tears in her eyes. She told me how her husband, an unbeliever, had worked alongside my father on the church roof. "Don't you get tired working up here every day?" her husband had asked my father.

"No," he replied with a twinkle in his eye and in his Norwegian accent. "When I'm working, I think about my best friend, Jesus, and everything He's done for me."

The lady brushed away a tear. "Because of your father, my husband committed his life to the Lord."

*Lord, may I build my life on things that count for You, so that regardless of my age, I will radiate Your love to others. Amen.*

Audrey Barcus enjoys writing mystery short stories. She works as a substitute teacher in her local high school and says her favorite hobby is needlepoint. Audrey and her husband have five children and make their home in Canyon Country, California.

# God's Gift

**Millie Wright Barger**

*How precious also are thy thoughts
unto me, O God! how great is the sum
of them!* Psalm 139:17, *KJV*

Your husband is God's gift to you,"
proclaimed the speaker. His statement jolted me.

My spouse, who sometimes irritates me and
whose faults I clearly see, is God's gift to me? I
always thought I was God's gift to my husband—a
helpmeet—as Eve was for Adam. Never before had I
considered him as my gift from God.

As if he read my mind, the minister continued, "A
gift from God is something to be respected, loved,
and treasured. God doesn't give any bad gifts."

The words burned in my heart: *respect, love,
treasure. Some days that's almost impossible, Lord,* I
silently cried. How can I respect him when he's
grouchy and makes issues over little things, or when
he fails to live up to his promises? How can I love
him when he often criticizes me? And what does
treasure mean? Do I have to take care of him as I
would a precious jewel? I can't pack a big man in
cotton and tuck him away in a drawer or safety

deposit box! *I'm confused, Lord.*

A few minutes later the speaker prayed, "May you have enough little things to forgive each day to teach you longsuffering."

*Oh, now I get it.* Do I show longsuffering—fruit of the spirit—when my spouse, God's gift to me, aggravates me? Or when he becomes angry, am I gentle and soft-spoken? Do I take the responsibility to guard my relationship with him? Do I have an inner peace when trouble strikes our home?

God wants to bring out in me: "love, joy, peace, longsuffering, gentleness, goodness, faith, meekness, temperance" (Galatians 5:22-23).

What better way could He have chosen than to give me a mate who tests me in all these areas? God knows what—and who—I need in my life to help me grow spiritually! His thoughts toward me are kind, and His gift—my spouse—is right for me.

*Thank You, Father, for the gift of Your Son. Thank You also for Your loving wisdom in giving me a husband to challenge me to be more Christlike. Amen.*

Millie Wright Barger co-leads a Christian writers' group in her area and teaches writers' workshops as well as Bible studies. She has written numerous articles and two books. Millie enjoys crocheting, bowling, stamp collecting, and swimming. She and her husband have two married children and reside in Phoenix, Arizona.

# Ready to Share

**Eileen M. Berger**

*I have laid up thy word in my heart.*
Psalm 119:11, *RSV*

While baby-sitting my grandchildren the other day, I overheard a discussion as to who would be the good guy and who the bad for the game they were about to play. After much running, chasing, and yelling, they got to the point where good would triumph, but the five-year-old protested, "You can't shoot me or arrest me!"

"Why not?"

"Cause you didn't tell me about Jesus yet, so I never had the chance to know about Him and decide to be saved and be good."

Three-year-old Isaac cocked his head to one side while he considered that. "Okay," he agreed, "so I'll tell you." And the little fellow stood in our hallway sharing his version of the salvation story.

He included God's sending Jesus as a baby who grew up to be always helping and healing everyone. "Even bad people listened to him," he explained, "like

Zacchaeus, who was so little he couldn't see Jesus till he climbed a light pole [Isaac's words]. But when Jesus told him to come down, they became friends and Zacchaeus got good and stopped stealing."

He drew in a big breath as he worked out his "theology" and then proceeded to tell of Jesus' persecution, death on the cross, and rising again on Easter. "So, if you love Jesus, He'll help you be good," he finished. His brother agreed that's what he would do, and the boys happily went outside together.

I looked after them with a smile on my face but with a question in my mind. How well would I have done, presenting the message of salvation on the spur of the moment, were I challenged by a sinner to lead him into a saving knowledge of Jesus? How well have I succeeded in making the Word of the Lord so much a part of me that I can readily share it with others?

*Dear Father, please help me to read, study, and remember Your Word so it becomes a part of me, always there for guidance, help, encouragement, and sharing. Amen.*

Eileen M. Berger is a medical technologist and assists in the operation of their family-owned Christmas tree farm. She has written numerous articles and poems as well as two novels. Eileen enjoys reading and being with others. She is married, has three children and lives in Hughsville, Pennsylvania.

# No Bare Cupboards

**Delores Elaine Bius**

*I have been young, and now am old;*
*yet have I not seen the righteous*
*forever, nor his seed begging bread.*
Psalm 37:25, *KJV*

When my husband had to go on disability due to a heart condition, I envisioned our cupboards becoming as bare as Old Mother Hubbard's in the nursery rhyme.

Having raised five sons, our life-style had never been an affluent one. Yet we had always had a roof over our heads, clothes to wear, and food to eat.

Now, however, I knew that it would be at least six months before my husband would get a disability check. I thought by then our meager savings would have evaporated as quickly as steam from my teakettle.

Having had major surgery a short time earlier, and having an ongoing battle with arthritis, I knew that holding down a full-time job myself might be too much. Also, such a job would cut into the time I spent in my free-lance writing, which I considered a ministry.

Thus, I went about informing the Lord, from dawn 'til dusk, about our precarious financial position, as if He didn't already know the end from the beginning.

Then one day I came across the above verse. I reminded myself how He had seen us through many other catastrophes. For example, there were the times my husband's company went on strike or had big layoffs. There were times when unexpected expenses such as furnace and plumbing repairs and automobile breakdowns threatened to bankrupt us. Yet we had not gone under. Surely God would not let us down this time either.

As the days went on, bread we had cast upon the water began to return to us. A friend I had counselled through the mail sent me several books of postage stamps. One son and daughter-in-law invited us out to eat several times. Another son borrowed our car and filled the gas tank. A neighbor shared produce from her garden so we had fresh salads daily, and I seemed to always have ingredients for zucchini bread and carrot cake.

A daughter-in-law took me grocery shopping. When she noticed me passing up some of my usual items, she later bought them herself and surreptitiously put them in my kitchen cupboards.

It got so that every morning upon awakening, I would say, "Lord, what new blessing will come today? I feel like Elijah being fed by ravens."

We did make it through the six-month waiting period, and I found my faith strengthened more than ever.

*Thank You, Lord, for reminding me that You own the*

*cattle on a thousand hills. Help me to always trust You for my daily bread. Amen.*

Delores Elaine Bius has written over 900 articles. She is an instructor for Christian Writers' Institute and speaker at conferences and retreats. She enjoys reading, encouraging others in their writing, and teaching adult Sunday School. Delores and her husband have five sons and make their home in Chicago, Illinois.

# Guiding My Footsteps

**Patricia Bolen**

*The steps of a good man are ordered by the Lord: and he delighteth in his way.* Psalm 37:23, *KJV*

I watched as the tow-truck driver eased his rig out into traffic, pulling our car behind him. I stood there holding my husband's hand, yet feeling abandoned.

It was eight o'clock Monday morning, the first day of a three-day getaway. The afternoon before, we had driven five hours in a rainstorm to historic Savannah, Georgia. Just two blocks from the motel, our car had started sputtering, and we had barely made it into the motel parking lot.

"Tommy, what will we do if it takes several days for repairs?" I asked. "We don't know a single soul in Savannah."

He tried to reassure me, but I was worried.

Once in our room, I reread our Scripture for the day: "The steps of a good man are ordered by the Lord."

"God," I said aloud, "if You're ordering our steps, why is our car being towed?"

Meanwhile, Tommy scanned a brochure that described the city's points of interest. He discovered a riverfront shopping area within walking distance;

we decided to go there.

We browsed through a few quaint shops, then entered a candy store. As we walked toward a tempting display of chocolate fudge, we spotted a familiar face, then a second one.

"Nancy! Jim! Fancy meeting you here," I said. It was a surprise to see these former neighbors who now lived several hundred miles away. We had a reunion right there in the store as we recalled good times shared.

Later, back at the motel, I said, "God *has* been ordering our steps. He helped us make it through the rainstorm to the motel before our car quit running. He led us to visit a place where we could walk to some of the historic sites. And, then, He led us to old friends in the midst of a strange city."

That afternoon, when the mechanic returned our car, we realized another benefit. The defective auto part was still under warranty.

As I reflected later that night on the events of the past two days, I thanked God that He had been aware of our every step.

*Lord, help me to remember that You are always guiding my footsteps, even when I do not recognize it. Amen.*

Patricia Bolen is a free-lance writer and has had several articles published in magazines, newspapers, and newsletters. She enjoys working crossword puzzles and reading mysteries and humor. Patricia and her husband have two daughters and make their home in Orlando, Florida.

# Fine Tuned by the Master

**Catharine Brandt**

*Not to us, O Lord, not to us but to
your name be the glory, because of
your love and faithfulness.*
Psalm 115:1, *NIV*

In a bell foundry in Holland, I
watched workmen cast a bell destined to hang in a
steeple in America. My companion and I had thrilled
to the ringing of famous bells in European
cathedrals. Now we would watch the workmen cast a
small carillon bell.

Bell founders had prepared the inner and outer
clay molds following specifications for shape, size,
and tone. Then they dropped the bronze ingots into
an iron cauldron over the hottest fire, watching until
the bronze turned red, then white-hot. At a signal
from the master bell founder, workmen tipped the

cauldron, pouring the molten bronze between the two layers of the mold.

After a cooling process of several days, bell makers would carefully break the clay molds, revealing the bell. We saw this process performed on another bell made a day or two earlier.

Next the bell was put into a tuning machine where it was chipped and pared around the rim, until it had the exact pitch and tone specified by the master bell founder. Then an electrical machine buffed and polished the bell. Soon it would be shipped to America where it would be part of a carillon ringing in harmony with the other bells.

When the fires of daily life burn hot, I ask, "Lord, do I need to go through this burning experience?" Then I remember the bell foundry in Holland. To fashion the bell required the hottest fire to melt the bronze bricks. It took patterns or molds, chipping, paring, and burnishing. Finally, the bell emerged with a clear ringing tone, exactly the way the master founder had planned.

Impatience makes me ask, "Lord, why can't I bong right now?"

But God has specifications for what He wants me to become as His child. God hasn't promised a life without testing, without pain and suffering, disappointment and sorrow. How I react in the foundry of life can be a ringing witness to His love and faithfulness. My response to testing can reveal to others that I have put myself into the hand of the Master Planner of my life and that I want all praise and glory to go to my Maker.

*Lord God, let me be willing to submit to the fire, the chipping, and the polishing so that my discordant*

*sounds may grow into sweet music of praise to You.*
*Amen.*

Catharine Brandt has written eleven books and over 800
articles and short stores and has taught several writing
classes. Catharine enjoys reading, her bell collection, and
volunteering at nursing homes. She has a son and daughter
and several grandchildren and makes her home in
Minneapolis, Minnesota.

# *The Buggy Blessing*

**Connie Bretz**

*O give thanks unto the Lord; call*
*upon his name: make known his*
*deeds among the people.*
Psalm 105:1, *KJV*

We have no car, and my husband recently became partially blind. I've always been afraid of driving because I've been in so many accidents through the years. Going to the supermarket became a problem. I could ride my Raleigh® bike and tote some groceries in the backpack, or I could walk. Always, I tended to get too much and ended up with a sore back and legs. What to do? God would provide an answer.

One day I spotted the worn, gray, baby coach looking deserted in the shallow creek. It didn't look too bad. Curiosity nudged me, so I pushed the coach out of the water and took a second look. Not bad. A good brand, Thayer,® a deep leather body, decent brakes, and solid rubber tires with spring suspension. No stains or rips anywhere except for a gray California-shaped glob of mildew.

I cleaned it with hot vinegar and Dutch® Cleanser.

"What are you going to do with that?" my husband, Bob, asked.

"What do you think?" I retorted.

"Dirty laundry? Your teddy bear collection?"

I laughed at his good answers. "Nope, grocery shopping."

"You're kidding," he answered.

"Wait and see," I said.

"People will laugh at you," Bob warned.

"Maybe," I said, "but I really need a solution, and the Lord has sent me this buggy." Bob didn't say anything.

I pushed the buggy the eight blocks to the market. Since it was lightweight, I could go quickly, and I think a few passersby thought I was going too fast for an infant. They couldn't see inside the buggy, but I did notice them looking at me as if I were an atypical Grandma.

On my first trip, I was too embarrassed to push the coach inside the market, so I secured it to a hitching post with my bike lock.

On the second trip, I thought, *Why not push the buggy into the supermarket?* My gray steed did look odd in contrast to the yellow carts, but it held eight bags of groceries and glided smoothly past the checkout counter. I told the bagger to forget about bags, to just pack the buggy. She balked a little, paged her manager, and got the OK.

Some people stared; some people smiled. One woman complimented, "What a good idea!"

Bob and I have received much help from Christian friends at desperate times: money, food, a tank of oil. But this buggy solved a problem, allowed me to exercise while I shopped, and I thank God for it.

*Heavenly Father, You care for me and help solve my daily problems. Nothing escapes Your notice. Thank You. Amen.*

Connie Bretz has written numerous poems, articles, and devotionals and has taught several writing classes. She enjoys biking, storytelling, collecting bells, and reading. Connie and her husband have four grown children and make their home in Phoenixville, Pennsylvania.

# *Memories: Lighting the Way*

**Sandra D. Bricker**

*For You will light my lamp; the Lord
my God will enlighten my darkness.*
Psalm 18:28, *NKJV*

I don't remember my father as a particularly God-fearing man; not during my childhood anyway. In fact, I vividly recall identifying with the Norman Rockwell portrait of the mom and kids trotting off to church while the dad remains behind, clad in robe and leather slippers, partaking of the Sunday news. My Dad wore those same kind of scuffed-up brown slippers.

"Say one for me," he would call out without even looking up, and we'd head off to church without him—except on holidays, that is, especially Christmas.

Before Christmas Eve services, it was our tradition, my dad's and mine—while Mom was off doing what only she could do in the kitchen and my brother was with the girlfriend of the season—to light the luminaria. Each house in the neighborhood would light candles inside paper bags filled with sand all along their properties. And once the winding roads of our little Ohio community were lined with flickering yellow lights, Dad and I would stand inside the garage of our red brick house atop the hill and admire our work. Towering over me from his 6-foot, 4-inch frame, he'd usually surround me with those big arms of his and whisper something like, "We did good, Baby." I waited all year for that moment.

"Why do we have the luminaria?" I asked him one year. I remember being startled at his reply.

"We're lighting the way," he said seriously. "Like the Lord's done for us."

I can't see a luminaria to this day, or make it through one Christmas season, without thinking of that night. I can remember what I was wearing, even the puppy my brother Terry had given his girlfriend Elaine. I can smell Mom's roast basting in its own juices, and I can still see that intensely serious look in my wonderful father's steel-blue eyes. It was my first glimpse of the spiritual side of my wise, beloved, sometimes tempestuous father, and I've never been able to shake it.

In later years he was in church every Sunday, and he prayed often. I'm grateful at the prospect of meeting up with him again once this world has passed away, and I look forward to losing myself for a time inside those strong arms I miss so much even now. But, mostly, I praise the Lord for the many times He has used that special Christmas memory to remind me that my way is lit and that He's in control, guiding me through.

*Thank You, Lord, for how You lead me and light my way. And thank You for using all those memories as ongoing reminders of Your sovereignty, of Your quiet intervention in my life, of Your perfect, abiding love.* Amen.


Sandra D. Bricker is the author of four books, one entitled *Dear Suzanne* (Evergreen, 1992). Sandie is also a free-lance screenwriter who enjoys needlework, ceramics, and long walks with her best buddy, a Sheepdog named Holly. She resides in Lake View Terrace, California.

# Consciousness Raising

**Thelma Brisbine**

*How precious also are thy thoughts
unto me, O God! how great is the sum
of them!* Psalm 139:17, *KJV*

I awoke to the familiar sound of an
airplane overhead. The digital clock by my bedside
read 5:40. I thought, *Yep, there goes Horizon, right on
schedule.* Just two months before, we had taken that
5:40 A.M. flight on the little twenty-passenger
commuter plane that connects our town to the big
airport in Seattle. It was the start of a trip south to
visit our son and his family, and the pleasant thirty-
five-minute jaunt by air would save us a three-hour
trip across the mountains by car.

The funny thing is that ever since our early
morning flight, I hear Horizon taking off at all times
of the day or evening. Now, that sound is nothing
new; Horizon has been making several trips a day
for years. What is new is that now I'm aware of the
sound. I've learned to differentiate Horizon's sound
from the sound of all of the other planes in the

area—the small, privately owned planes, the spray planes, the big jets that fly high overhead. I'll hear the distinctive drone of its motors as it ascends and heads out over the mountains to the west. I'll think, *There goes Horizon*, and for a moment I'm up there with it, feeling that exhilarating lift as we head for the clouds.

I guess you could say I've had my consciousness raised where Horizon is concerned. It was there all the time; I just hadn't heard it.

The thought occurs to me that this is what I need concerning my heavenly Father. His Word tells me that He has precious thoughts concerning me—thoughts that are constant, thoughts so numerous that they're like grains of sand. It boggles my mind. God thinks of me!

Oh, yes, I do want to have my consciousness raised to God's thoughts. They are there to bless, to guide. As I go about my daily routine, as I read my Bible, as I interact with people, I want to hear His voice. I need His wisdom. Just as I've become aware of the sound of a certain airplane above all the others, I want to tune in to God's voice, to think His thoughts, to feel the exhilaration of being lifted into His presence.

*Dear Lord, thank You that amid the many voices in the world today, Your voice may still be heard if I listen. Your thoughts toward me are precious. Amen.*

Thelma Brisbine has had several of her articles and poems published. Besides writing she enjoys reading, gardening, and entertaining. Thelma and her husband, Waldo, have five sons. The Brisbines make their home in Wenatchee, Washington.

# Windows to Heaven

**Mary J. Brown**

*Yea, thou dost light my lamp; the*
*Lord my God lightens my darkness.*
Psalm 18:28, *RSV*

Last summer I accompanied my
scientist husband, Alex, to the University of
Stellenbosch in South Africa. As we strolled across
campus to meet Alex's colleague, Werner, the silver
tops of the nearby mountains glistened in the
sunlight. Swaying palm trees beckoned us to enjoy
the day outdoors.

But we had work to complete, so when we met
Werner I said, "If you'll direct me to the nearest
library, I'll leave you fellows to your physics."

"Oh, yes," he said, "we have a marvelous library
and it's all underground."

*Underground*, I thought dismally. I had pictured
working by a window overlooking one of the lovely
stone courtyards filled with cranberry-colored
bougainvilleas. Instead I resigned myself to being

submerged in a dreary, fluorescent-lit tomb of books and scholars.

However, as I descended to the reference section on the bottom floor, the rooms became brighter. Potted palms and fig trees flourished under a skylight. One entire wall was glass, and the study tables overlooked flowers and fountains. I marveled at the architecture. Here I was three stories underground with sunlight streaming across my desk.

It struck me that my life on earth is, in a sense, underground—sealed away from heaven's splendor. It would be a dark, dreary existence, except my loving Father gives me His light. I can design my days to allow God's grace to shine into my soul by including times of prayer and Bible reading, by serving others, and by pausing to reflect on His love.

As I worked in that pleasant library, I was inspired to open my life to more of God's light. Each time I thank Him, take His Word into my heart, respond in love to someone, or look for His presence in daily events, I'm opening a window to heaven.

*Lord, help me see the light of Your love and presence each day. Amen.*

Mary J. Brown is a homemaker, free-lance writer, and speaker. She enjoys singing, playing the piano, gardening, walking, and family bike riding. Mary has traveled extensively with her husband who is a professor at Michigan State University. The Browns have one daughter and live in East Lansing, Michigan.

# Without A Trace

**Sharon Broyles**

*Happy the man whose fault is
forgiven, whose sin is blotted out.*
Psalm 32:1, *JB*

Yuk!" I said to my husband as we
stood poolside peering into the murky mess. "It'll
never happen. We'll have to drain the pool and start
all over. No amount of chemicals will clean up this
swamp."

We hadn't been as vigilant as we might have been
through the winter. The plastic pool cover had found
it's way into our large in-ground swimming pool
bringing with it all manner of leaves and debris,
until the water was not just dirty, but completely
and thoroughly putrid. By April, it was so black and
slimy, we could see our reflections in it. I was
scowling and feeling not a little embarrassed. *What
would the neighbors think*? Marvin's face was
unreadable. He was lost in thought.

"You just wait," he finally announced to a
doubting me. "We'll swim in here yet."

Thus began a cleansing process that took more than three weeks and twice our annual pool budget. Marvin started dumping chemicals into what I was sure would never be clean water again. Then he got the pump going to keep the stagnant scum moving through a filtering process. Pretty soon I could make out the first step. Eventually, a thick layer of leaves that had settled at the bottom was barely visible. We "volunteered" the kids and they started scooping out nets full of decayed leaves and dead bugs and an occasional lifeless rodent. It was hard, time-consuming, sweaty, smelly, expensive work requiring bushels of patience.

Marvin was right. We did swim and play in that same water—water once stagnant, now clear and shimmering, sparkling in the summer sun. Only months before, most people, especially me, would have thought it impossible to clean up that mess.

This experience reminds me of God's transformation process at work in me. First He uncovered the swampy mess that I am. Then He patiently set out to cleanse me—with the blood of His Son—to make me a source of refreshment to others.

*Oh, God, I'm so glad You know just how to make me eternally happy. Please help me yield to Your present-day work in me. Amen.*

Sharon Broyles is a free-lance writer who has received several awards for her poetry, fiction, and personal experience writing. She enjoys needlework, reading, and working word puzzles. Sharon and her husband, Marvin, have three children and reside in Hagerstown, Maryland.

# Cleaning Blackboards

**Elisabeth Buddington**

*As far as the east is from the west, so
far has he removed our transgressions
from us.* Psalm 103:12, *NIV*

Of all the ways of "helping
teacher," cleaning the blackboards was the job most
prized by us fourth and fifth graders. I remember
how the teacher would rotate classroom chores so
that for a week at a time we got to end the afternoon
by erasing, with great sweeping movements, the
day's work from the faded, old blackboards. Feeling
important, we would climb onto a chair to reach the
topmost corners.

Then, best of all, we took the erasers outdoors to
clean them by clapping them soundly against each
other. What fun to be outside, creating billows of
chalky clouds!

Finally, on Friday, we washed those blackboards.
Proudly we eliminated each smudge and stroke with
our dripping sponges. Now the slate was clean, the

past week gone, and it was ready for a brand new week.

I like to think that God's forgiveness is like that. As each day goes on, mistakes, sins, regrets, and slip-ups accumulate. When I confess these and ask His pardon, He wipes the slate clean with large, powerful strokes. If I take a few moments at bedtime for this cleansing, I can go to sleep freed from the day's dusty remains.

Beyond the erasing, God washes the slate of my life so thoroughly that, in His eyes, not a trace of the guilt can be seen or even remembered. I don't have to suffer from unresolved remorse or a guilty conscience. Each Sunday when I join my fellow Christians in corporate worship, I am renewed and refreshed by that reminder. Like the weekly washing of those long-ago blackboards, the weekly fellowship with God and His people gives me a fresh new beginning for the dawning week.

*I need to know that my transgressions have been removed, Lord. How kind You are to give this assurance in Your Word. Thank You. Amen.*

Elisabeth Buddington is a coordinator for the Christian Writers' Fellowship in Springfield, Massachusetts. Her devotions and articles have appeared in numerous publications. Besides writing she enjoys music. Elisabeth is married, has three grown children and makes her home in East Longmeadow, Massachusetts.

# The Gift
# of Grace

**Georgia E. Burkett**

*The Lord is nigh unto all them that
call upon him, to all that call upon
him in truth.* Psalm 145:18, *KJV*

I've got to get out of here," I told
myself. "If I fall asleep during Susan's presentation,
I'll never be able to face her as long as I live."

We were just completing an exciting, but hectic,
two-day writers' conference, and I felt as though I
had been put through a wringer. I could feel my
shoulders slumping down like melting candles, and
every time I yanked open my drooping eyelids, they
slid down again. So, to avoid making a spectacle of
myself, I quietly slipped out the back door of the
crowded room. "If only I can find a secluded spot
where I can rest for a few minutes," I reasoned,
"maybe I can pull myself together."

God surely knew how I felt, for He had one of His
"ministering angels" out in the hallway waiting for
me. "Come, Georgia," she whispered quietly as she
guided me to a chair, "sit here and relax while I rub
your back."

Gratefully, I breathed deep as Grace gently, but
firmly, massaged my aching muscles. A few minutes
later she placed her hands on my head, and I could
sense that she was silently asking the Lord to revive
my strength.

God answered Grace's prayer, for I was soon ready to return to the meeting as refreshed as though I had enjoyed a good nap. But even before I rose from the chair, Grace was reaching out to another haggard escapee from the conference room. I couldn't help wondering how many other weary backs she might have rubbed that day.

The Psalmist said that the Lord is nigh unto them that call upon Him. And He gives special fruits, listed in Galatians 5:22-23, to those who live close to Him—gentleness and goodness included. Grace is not hesitant to use her share of those gifts, but it is easy to see that she depends on God to show her how.

Later that evening I remembered Grace's comforting hands as she massaged my back and how close to the Lord I felt when she placed her hands on my head. What a blessing I felt.

"If only I, too, could be one of Your ministers of comfort," I told God.

"You can," I seemed to hear Him answer. "Just open your eyes and your heart. Depend on Me, and I'll tell you what to do."

*Lord, I do want to help relieve sadness and pain, but all too often I'm lazy and unresponsive to the needs of others. Please forgive me, and help me to have a servant's heart and willing hands. Amen.*

Georgia E. Burkett has written numerous articles and devotionals and has received several writing awards. She recently organized the Harrisburg Area Christian Writers' Fellowship. Besides writing she enjoys gardening, reading, and needlework. Georgia has six children and makes her home in Middletown, Pennsylvania.

# To Be Desired

**Sue Cameron**

*The precepts of the Lord are right,
rejoicing the heart ... More to be
desired are they than gold, even than
much fine gold; sweeter also than
honey and the drippings from the
honeycomb.* Psalm 19:8,10, *AMP*

Mom, can you make me a piece of toast?"
"Mom, where's my homework?"
"Mom, I can't find my shoes."

"Children," I explain in a calm, controlled
manner, "I have to get your little brother and myself
ready for Bible study."

But as I mount the stairs the chorus follows me,
"But I need ... and I want ... and you have to ..." So I
turn around and stomp down the stairs.

By the time my older children are off to school, I
only have a few minutes before I need to leave. My
curious three- year-old asks, "Mommy, why are you
getting the vacuum?"

"Because," I growl, "we have company coming

here for lunch, and there is cereal all over the rug. I've got to hurry or I'll be late for Bible study, and you'll be late for story hour."

That's when the thought sneaks into my mind: *You don't have to go to Bible study today; after all, you're tired. You got to bed at midnight and woke up extra early. Why push yourself so hard?*

"Maybe," I suggest to my youngest, "we'll just stay home."

"No, Mommy! I want to go." His crying increases to a howl, "I want to go, please!"

We rush out to the car. I am frazzled when we reach church. I quickly settle my son upstairs. Piano music is playing as I slip in and join the singing.

"Jesus, name above all names, beautiful Savior, glorious Lord ..."

Then, deep within me in my very middle, I know that this is where I belong. This is what I long for. All the rest of life with its clutter and busyness is not to be compared with this moment.

And when we meditate on God's Word, I am filled with strong joy. It feeds me, nourishes me, changes me. I rediscover that His Word is sweeter than honey and more desirable than gold. I return home filled to overflowing.

*Lord, remind me of this day when I'm tempted to give other things top priority. Help me obey when I hear You call me away for a quiet moment of fellowship. Amen.*

Sue Cameron enjoys writing, baking bread, and sacred dance. She also likes to travel, which she says is a good thing since her husband, Craig, is an United States Army physician. The Camerons have four children and currently make their home in Heidelberg, Germany.

# Nora's Gift

### Suzanne P. Campbell

*For thou dost bless the righteous, O
Lord; thou dost cover him with favor
as with a shield.* Psalm 5:12, *RSV*

Nora, an elderly friend of my
grandmother's, was always considered part of the
family. A woman of deep faith, she lived frugally in a
small apartment in the city and traveled by bus, her
old black leather handbag sitting on her lap.

When we invited her to our wedding, she
accepted with joy. Somehow in all the plans and
preparations, each person thought another had
arranged for Nora's transportation. It was the fall of
1966 and summer had been a time of tension. Race
riots filled even our normally placid midwestern city
with hatred and frustration. We had all taken to
traveling with our car doors locked.

Nora decided to get to the wedding by herself.
She boarded a bus at 5:30 P.M., not daunted by the
thought of traveling alone through the city for more
than an hour into unfamiliar territory. "I made a
mistake and got off at the wrong place," she
explained later at the reception. "But that was all

right, because I stopped at a house and asked the people there what I should do."

We could picture the scene: The young man answering the door in the gathering twilight to discover a seventy-eight-year-old woman in a well-worn coat, an old-fashioned velvet hat pinned securely to her wispy white hair and a wedding gift in her hands.

She continued the story. "He said, 'Stay right there; I'll get the car and drive you to the church. It's much too far to walk and it's getting dark.' So here I am; wasn't that nice?"

We lectured her about the dangers of traveling alone at night and of asking strangers for help. She wouldn't hear of it. "I prayed, and God has always taken care of me before. Why should He stop now?" she asked, her faded blue eyes glowing.

Nora's most important wedding gift to us that day wasn't the carefully wrapped package of knitted dishcloths. It was her witness to almost eight decades of living with a God she could trust.

*Thank You, Lord, for the memory of Nora's gift. After more than twenty years, I know it's one of the most important we received. Help me to continue trusting even when the way is not clear. Amen.*

Suzanne P. Campbell has written over 200 articles, devotionals and scripts, belongs to the Minnesota Christian Writers' Guild, and works as a volunteer mentor for young writers. Suzanne enjoys traveling and hosting international guests. She and her husband have two teenagers and reside in Minneapolis, Minnesota.

# God Wasn't Surprised

### Tricia Canafax-Wade

*O Lord, you have searched me and
you know me. You know when I sit
and when I rise; you perceive my
thoughts from afar. You discern my
going out and my lying down; you are
familiar with all my ways.*
Psalm 139:1-3, *NIV*

Your heart has compensated all it
can. The pressure in your lungs is high, and the
condition is irreversible. Our goal now is to keep you
from getting worse."

The doctor was kind and caring, yet the words
were hard to hear. I had been diagnosed with
pulmonary hypertension, high blood pressure in the
arteries of the lungs. Instead of the normal pressure
of 25, mine was 85. Having gone through difficult
times before and knowing the power and
compassionate heart of the God I had accepted as
Lord and Savior some twelve years ago, I knew this
had not caught God off guard, as it had me.

While unexpected, the condition was
understandable. As a small child, I had had open
heart surgery. The main problem was corrected, and
now, some thirty-four years later, a side effect had
shown itself. While not immediately life threatening,
my life-style was indeed undergoing change. Simple

61

tasks had slowly become major chores, until I found that some days merely washing a load of laundry was all I could do without having to rest or nap.

I longed for the energy to read pages and pages of God's life-giving Word, yet would read only a few sentences before falling asleep. In half-waking, half-sleeping moments, I would try to recall some of the special Scriptures that had become a bond between my Lord and me.

Psalm 139 kept coming to mind. I lay in bed, desperately trying to remember the words. "Search me, O God, and know my heart; test me and know my anxious thoughts. See if there is any offensive way in me, and lead me in the way everlasting," were my heart's prayer. I knew that God spoke very clearly on where the origin of life begins, in the mother's womb. Yet I could not shake the need to read the Psalm. I reached for my Bible, turned on the light, and started to read. When I reached the third verse, I began to weep. "You discern my going out and my lying down; you are familiar with all my ways."

No, my recent diagnosis had not caught God by surprise. He knew every movement—and lack of movement—I made. And He showed me that He was indeed going through this difficult time with me.

*Thank You, Lord, for the comfort of knowing that You are not surprised by life's circumstances and that You are always there to help me though them. Amen.*

Tricia Canafax-Wade loves traveling and the outdoors. She and her husband spent eight months traveling and camping across the United States. In addition, Tricia has served as a chore provider for senior citizens. The Wades have one son and make their home in Leavenworth, Washington.

# Rest in God

**Barbara Caponegro**

*My soul finds rest in God alone; my*
*salvation comes from him.*
Psalm 62:1, *NIV*

My first instinct was to run from
the hospital room. The stale stagnant air made my
lungs strain to breathe. To keep my eyes from the
frail man lying in bed, I eyed the wilted flowers by
the telephone and water pitcher.

As his wife bent over to talk to him, I heard her
arthritic bones talk of a life long lived. She
whispered encouragement and love in his ear. He
responded with a slight muscle twinge on his face.

The years had been good to them—all fifty-five of
them. Having had no children, they were everything
to each other. She wept, knowing that loneliness
would be her new companion.

The nurse rushed in to adjust his oxygen mask
and offer us empty words of hope. With her footsteps
gone, all that was heard was the labored breathing of
an old man so close to the end. The doctors could do
no more. I shifted nervously, not knowing what to do
or say. I prayed quietly. All this was new to me:

waiting for answered prayer, waiting for death.

Time passed. I reflected on the wisdom of God's Word about His being our hope and comfort. I imagined myself in that deathbed, waiting for the end. And I realized how precious my salvation was! I had no fear of crossing over. The saving grace of salvation will overcome any sickness, disease, or disaster. It is our passport in transporting our souls to heaven … the final destination. How empty to pass without a ticket.

Interrupting her vigil, his wife left the room. I remained. He stirred and wanted water. As he sipped I thought about the eternal water that Jesus promises us. Another reason to give thanks amid this sadness.

I was new to this wisdom, and there was so much my heart wanted to say to him. Again I prayed, but for bold words filled with everlasting hope, words to comfort him. "Uncle Alfred, do you believe in Jesus?" His eyes opened wide. "Can I pray with you?"

Instead of silent empty hope, the room was filled with sounds of eternal joy as he affirmed his love for the Lord! He wanted to confess and did so in his heart, a private conversation between Uncle Alfred and His Savior whom he soon would see.

She came back into the room and saw my tears. Her arms embracing me, she wept too. But my tears were joyful ones. I was too overcome to explain it; there would be time during the ride home.

I watched her adjust the pillow, tuck in the covers and say good-bye to him. How was she to know that his comfort was not only in these small kindnesses, but also in Jesus who was already handing him his ticket to eternity.

*Father, Your salvation is a precious gift. Thank You for the rest and comfort it brings. Amen.*

Barbara Caponegro is a former first grade and nursery school teacher. Besides writing she enjoys reading, traveling, cooking, and counted cross-stitch. Barbara and her husband, Pat, have two children and make their home in Medford, New Jersey.

# A Level Path

**Jan Carpenter**

*Teach me Thy way, O Lord, and lead
me in a level path, because of my foes.*
Psalm 27:11, *NASB*

I live with chronic pain. Although
the intensity of the pain varies, it is nevertheless
with me twenty-four hours a day, seven days a week!

At first I was full of anger and self-pity. Then fear
took over. I was afraid to make a commitment I
might not be able to fulfill. Any kind of shopping
filled me with dread, because sometimes the pain
would become so intense that I would leave the items
I intended to purchase and stagger out the door,
wondering how I would ever be able to drive home.

The only drugs that relieved my anguish were
addicting and mind altering and could not be taken
on a regular basis. Heeding the advice of my trusted
doctor, I checked into a hospital pain clinic, where I
lived for the next month, attending classes and
participating in various exercises. It helped to know
and share with others who were suffering as I was,
but I still hurt.

Like the apostle Paul, I cried out over and over
again to God, pleading with Him to remove the pain.
It didn't happen. I felt as if I were on the outside
looking in when I had to say no to my friends who
invited me to join them in sports such as cross-
country skiing. I tried taking walks, but even that

was torture and I would be in tears before I made it home.

Finally, one day in desperation, I screamed out to the Lord, "I give up, I'm tired of fighting—I give in. If there's something you want me to learn from all this, please show me."

Lightning didn't strike, but something different did begin to happen. I learned to relax and be still. After being a Martha all of my life, I related to Mary for the first time. I began to listen to the Lord.

Now, sometimes I can sit quietly without becoming tense and I'm starting to see God's touch in everything around me. I feel His presence in the birds feeding outside my kitchen window; the red cardinals remind me of the Holy Spirit. And instead of resenting rain, I take pleasure in it. Many times, through my writing, I am lifted out of my agony. I even have moments when I almost appreciate the suffering. It no longer has a hold over me.

No, I still don't like this affliction that is with me twenty-four hours a day, but I am grateful for what I am learning through it. Now, not only do I savor and appreciate everything that God has made, but best of all, I am learning to hear my Savior's voice!

*Dear Lord Jesus, forgive my stubbornness and thank You for never giving up on me. Help me to listen. I love You. Amen.*

Jan Carpenter has written numerous devotions, including her own devotional book. In addition to writing, she enjoys music, volunteering at a nursing home, and being a grandmother. Jan is a former preschool teacher, is married and has two grown children. She and her husband, Jim, make their home in Orono, Minnesota.

# Simple Gifts

**Lynn Casale**

*The Lord is close to the brokenhearted
and saves those who are crushed in
spirit.* Psalm 34:18, *NIV*

I hung up the phone and burst
into tears. I had just received word that a close
friend had died after a lengthy illness; my grief rose
quickly and powerfully to the surface and washed
over me.

Soon I became aware that I was not alone. My
two-year-old daughter Sarah was quietly observing
me, her eyes clouded with concern. After a moment's
thoughtful reflection, she wordlessly offered me
something which had often brought her great comfort
in her own times of distress and sadness.

She offered me her thumb.

In the stillness, as we cuddled together, I thought
about how her quiet act of love embodied for me the
meaning of 2 Corinthians 1:4, that God "comforts us
in all our troubles, so that we can comfort those in
any trouble with the comfort we ourselves have
received from God." While God expresses His comfort
to us in many different ways, through Scripture or a

song, in prayer or meditation, it seems that He often mends our broken hearts through another person; His Spirit within them ministers to our own spirit and we can sense the nearness of God. This comfort then can bear fruit, and we, in turn, can offer it to another who is hurting.

Many times I feel inadequate to meet the needs of a person in pain and wish that I could give some word that would ease their suffering. But frequently what is needed is that I humbly offer myself, as Sarah did. By His grace, God can manifest consolation to one of His children through me, in my quiet presence, my warm embrace, and my faithful intercession.

These simple gifts—a visit, a hug, and a prayer to the "Father of compassion and the God of all comfort" (2 Corinthians 1:3)—are a healing balm for a wounded soul.

*Lord, thank You for Your nearness to me in times of sorrow and for the people You have used to reveal Your love to me. I am available to You today to pass along that comfort to someone else who hurts. Amen.*

Lynn Casale besides writing enjoys reading, journaling, cooking, singing, and volunteering at school. In addition, she is involved in a ministry to women abused as children. Lynn and her husband, Jeff, have two daughters and make their home in Oakland, California.

# 'Tis a Gift to Be Simple

**Amelia Chaffee**

*I love the Lord, for he heard my voice;
he heard my cry for mercy ... I was
overcome by trouble and sorrow. Then
I called on the name of the Lord: "O
Lord, save me!" The Lord is gracious
and righteous; our God is full of
compassion. The Lord protects the
simplehearted.* Psalm 116:1-6, *NIV*

When my children were small, I had the privilege of staying home with them, and we had a glorious time making mud pies. As my moppets entered kindergarten, however, I wanted more intellectually stimulating company, so I too enrolled in school.

I loved my classes; it was exciting to be surrounded by people who had more meaningful discussions than whether we would watch "Sesame Street" or "The Electric Company." Gradually I looked forward more and more to my times of escape into the grown-up world of ideas and found myself resenting the hours I spent washing sticky floors and making peanut butter sandwiches.

One afternoon, troubled by a nagging sense that I was losing my perspective, I set out to meet the kids at school with my German shepherd, Bear, tagging along.

"Father," I cried out to God as we loped down the street, "I feel so trapped. Where is the creativity in reading the same story for the 407th time? It seems as if nothing I do matters. Please show me what's really important!"

Then a group of children rode by on their bikes. One little girl, trying to stop too fast, fell off and scraped her knee. I started toward her, but her brother got there first. Gently he picked her up; comforted, she rode off with the others.

As I watched this unexpected show of compassion, it was as though a wave broke through the fog: kindness. Kindness mattered.

We reached the corner where the crossing guard awaited his charges. He shyly beckoned for me to come see an ornate box he had carved. Now Mr. Roberts, a kindly, grandfatherly sort of man, had faithfully seen my children safely across that street for five years, but he had picked that day to share his treasure with me. As Bear and I crossed the street, another wave of understanding hit me: people. People mattered. I realized that God had given me a crash course in what really is important.

Suddenly I couldn't wait for my children to come running out of their classrooms so we could walk home together. We would greet all the dogs and cats we met along the way and pick a bouquet of wild flowers for Grandma. Then we would dunk graham crackers in milk until they turned to mush and had to be eaten with a spoon ... and read Winnie-the-

Pooh for the 408th time. And we'd love it!

*Forgive me, Lord, for being discontent with my life and rebelling against the place You put me. Help me to enjoy the simple things You provide for me, and don't let me forget what truly matters. Amen.*

Amelia Chaffee is a free-lance writer, the author of several articles. Besides writing she enjoys working with youth, producing newsletters and flyers, and singing. Amelia and her husband have two teenagers and make their home in Ventura, California.

# A Love Bath

**Kitty Chappell**

*Cease striving and know that I am
God; ... I will be exalted in the earth.*
Psalm 46:10, *NASB*

Yesterday I bathed my two cats in a nontoxic flea solution. Smokey spit and scratched me, making the job not only more difficult but twice as long and hard on both of us. Cinco struggled and cried for a few moments. Then with sad eyes fixed intently upon my face, he laid his head on the side of my arm and yielded.

My eyes filled with tears as I realized the truth of the moment. I should be more like Cinco and less like Smokey. How I struggle and fight when uncomfortable! I recalled bitter disappointments when things hadn't gone the way I'd wanted, specifically that "perfect" job I had wanted where all of the employees were Christians. But no, I had been hired by a firm where I was the only Christian. How I struggled to get out of that situation—an office steeped in immorality, including drug and alcohol abuse.

I had given my notice but agreed to stay until I found another job. Though I received the highest ratings on tests and interviews, it was as though some force were holding me back. I cried out to God and was told to be still. I went on more job interviews and each night lashed out with sharp complaints. I searched God's Word for some reason for His firmness, and I began to notice a pattern.

"Love your neighbor as yourself" (Matthew 19:19); "If God so loved us, we also ought to love one another" (1 John 4:11); and finally, "It is not those who are healthy who need a physician, but those who are sick" (Mark 2:17).

I complained that although my co-workers liked me, I was uncomfortable there for I had nothing in common with them. God's Word showed me how wrong I was. "While we were yet sinners, Christ died for us" (Romans 5:8), and "There is not a righteous man on earth who never sins" (Ecclesiastes 7:20).

At last I had yielded and let God fill me with love for an office in which He was ultimately exalted— through the reflection of His love and truth—in me.

I glanced at Smokey, who sulked in the far corner of the kitchen, and recalled how I, too, had resisted what I thought was a bad experience. I now know that God gave me exactly what I needed by not giving me what I wanted, when He gave me His love bath.

*Lord, help me in difficult times to lay my head against You and trust You completely. Amen.*

Kitty Chappell is a speaker and writer of several articles, devotions, and poems. Her book on friendship will be released by Evergreen in 1992. She enjoys rose gardening, downhill skiing, teaching college age Sunday School classes, and collecting antiques. Kitty and her husband have a grown son and daughter and make their home in Ojai, California.

# Trust in the Lord

**Joan Clayton**

*But let all those that put their trust
in thee rejoice: let them ever shout for
joy, because thou defendest them: let
them also that love thy name be joyful
in thee.* Psalm 5:11, *KJV*

I awakened at three o'clock in the
morning. Immediately the anxiety returned. My
mother was very ill. At eighty-three, her tired, frail
little body was trying desperately to hold on. In just
three hours I would have to get up and go to my
second graders, a job I love, but somehow the
thought kept plaguing me, *Can we keep her at home
and give her the care she needs?*

Sleep eluded me until I regained control by
repeating my favorite Scriptures: "All things work
together for good ... trust in the Lord with all thine
heart ... I can do all things through Christ." The next
thing I knew it was five-thirty in the morning.

About nine-thirty that morning a man appeared
in my doorway at school. He was the father of a child

I had had the year before.

"Mrs. Clayton," he began, "I don't know how to tell you this, but I awakened this morning at three o'clock with a real burden to pray for you. So I just got up and prayed for you. And then I made you a cake." In his arms was this beautifully decorated cake that read "God bless you Mrs. Clayton."

I cried and told him of my earlier morning experience.

"Well," he said, as he turned to leave, "I just want to be obedient and sensitive to the Spirit's leading. I shall continue to pray for you. And I hope this cake will give you a lift and brighten your day!"

Talk about a lift. Besides the delicious cake, the fact that this man sacrificed by arising at three o'clock in the morning to pray for me brought me to my knees.

We have such a loving Savior. He raised up an intercessor for me at my point of deepest need. I received the peace, and my mother received the healing.

I will trust in the Lord!

*Dear Father, thank You for this man who was sensitive to Your nudging to pray for me. And thank You most of all for the One who intercedes daily on my behalf, Your Son Jesus. Amen.*

Joan Clayton has been published in several magazines. Besides writing, she enjoys oil painting, gardening, playing the piano, and sweatshirt painting. In addition, she teaches in the public schools. Joan is married, has three sons, and makes her home in Portales, New Mexico.

# What Do You Do With the Pain?

## J. Martha Compleman

*He put a new song in my mouth, a
hymn of praise to our God. Many will
see and fear and put their trust in the
Lord. Psalm 40:3, NIV*

Tears blurred my vision as I tried
to concentrate on the road ahead. My foot on the
accelerator propelled the blue Volkswagon bug
relentlessly toward an 8:00 A.M. class. After twenty
years of childrearing, I was again enrolled in college.
My college-age son was not. I did not even know
where he was.

How long had I been carrying this agonizing hole
within myself? Only three days—since he walked out
late at night with a few belongings and his guitar? It
seemed a lifetime.

Strange. After a long season of father-son
conflicts, it was after a sharp clash with me that he

left. I didn't know I could hurt so much, that a damaged relationship could generate such pain.

"God!" I cried aloud. "What do you do with the pain?"

The Volkswagon churned on. My attention shifted. I thought of a poem I had written many years ago and a tune appeared out of nowhere. They came together. My mouth opened and I sang a new song: a song of God's love for my son; a song of being a child of God. Pain was released. Despair gave way to wonder—wonder at the loving provision of my God.

I parked and walked to class wrapped in the embrace of God's releasing creative energy, secure in the knowledge that His love is adequate.

After class, I walked down one corridor, turned into another, and there by the building entrance stood my son, waiting to see me.

The new dimension in music remained; song continued. As family relationships strained and then improved, song deepened into prayer and praise to be shared with others.

*Lord Jesus, into Your hands I loose my pain, my grief. Into Your hands I release rebellion, anger, guilt, and shame. Amen.*

J. Martha Compleman has completed a Master of Divinity degree at Fuller Seminary. She writes reviews and newspaper and magazine articles. She has four grown sons and seven grandchildren and makes her home in Mesa, Arizona.

# *Facing Fear*

**Pauline E. Cramer**

*God is our refuge and strength, an
ever-present help in trouble.*
Psalm 46:1, *NIV*

**M**y hand trembled as I shoved
open the barn door and stepped inside. Half praying
and half complaining under my breath, I whispered
to the dusty silence, "How will I manage our ranch
with my husband gone for a whole month? If only we
could have made ends meet. I guess I should be
thankful he found some temporary work to pay the
bills."

I took a deep breath and tried to shake the
feelings of fear that controlled my thinking. As I
walked toward the pasture, I repeated the words of
the Psalmist and clutched at the promise: "God is
our refuge and strength, an ever-present help in
trouble."

I leaned against the fence and tried to calm my
mind by watching my quarter horse contentedly
grazing at the far end of the pasture. His sorrel coat
glistened in the morning sunlight. Each muscle and
bone of his body was finely balanced for strength and

speed. Blended with his sturdy frame was a gentle temperament. Butterflies dipped and fluttered around the huge animal as testament to his genial nature. I remembered the times I'd wrapped my arms around his stout neck, giving him a loving hug, or clinging to him in tears wanting to absorb his strength. He always accepted me. He merely stood there quiet and patient, ready to carry the weight of my troubles as well as my body.

Yet, I know that any moment, this gentle friend has the capability to turn into a powerhouse of danger. With one swift kick he can end my life or cripple me. My abilities are minute next to his. Even though I love my horse, I'm aware of his power and respect his strength. Somehow that always helps me understand how I can love God and yet also fear and reverence Him at the same time.

"Jessie!" I called to my horse. His head bobbed up at the sound of my voice. With slow, careful steps he moved toward me. "God must be like that," I told my nagging fears. I'm His child and He knows the sound of my voice. Why did I allow fear to build a fence between us? He's waiting to help me with His loving and gentle power. All I have to do is call His name.

*Lord, thank You for walking beside me each day and helping me overcome my fears. Amen.*

Pauline E. Cramer besides writing enjoys cooking, baking bread, camping, hiking, and tending her large herb garden. She and her husband, Judd, have two grown children and make their home on a cattle ranch in the Rocky Mountains in Challis, Idaho.

*May God supply all your needs —*
*Love, Elaine Cunningham*

# He Supplies Our Needs

**Elaine Cunningham**

*The lions may grow weak and hungry, but those who seek the Lord lack no good thing.* Psalm 34:10, *NIV*

I know that God supplies the needs of His children. Back in the fifties my husband pastored a small church in Florida. Our two children were toddlers; John, three, and Ruth, two. One Friday we realized that the milk was gone and we had no money to buy more. Our home mission salary seemed never to stretch far enough. We knew that our babies needed milk so we knelt down and asked God to supply our need.

In our desperation we claimed the promises of God. "You said in Your Word, Lord, that we would lack no good thing." We prayed, making our request known to Him.

We were still on our knees praying when the doorbell rang. Our next-door neighbor stood with two gallon jugs of milk in her hands.

"I feel foolish asking, but could you possibly use

some extra milk?" she hesitatingly asked. "Our milkman left this and we're going away for the weekend."

"You're the quickest answer to prayer I've ever seen," I answered.

Coincidence? Perhaps. But can you think of better timing for one of those God-planned happenings in the lives of His children! We will probably never know the many times God has intervened in our situations. I have learned to trust Him daily. Those who seek the Lord lack no good thing.

*Lord, help me to never forget that You are there when I need You. Thank You for supplying all my needs. Amen.*

Elaine Cunningham has written two books and numerous articles and short stories. Besides writing she enjoys reading and music. Elaine and her husband, Cloyce, have two grown children and make their home in Wenatchee, Washington.

# To Choke or Grant Mercy

**Kay David**

*You have laid down precepts that are*
*to be fully obeyed. Oh, that my ways*
*were steadfast in obeying your*
*decrees!* Psalm 119:4-5, *NIV*

What's for dinner?" my twenty-year-old son asked after a day at work.

"What's for dinner?" I scorned. "Why not, 'Hi, Mom, how was your day?' for a change?"

Lately my reactions to my son had been razor sharp. I often felt the urge to choke him. If only he would do more chores, wear his helmet while riding his motorcycle, or be more friendly.

In my mind, I pushed aside any creeping doubts that my reactions were wrong, that I contributed to the problem.

Then one summer day, I erupted to my husband. "I have had enough of these injustices. In two days, we *will* have a family meeting and straighten this son out." I hoped that in two days my volcanic spirit would lose some steam. However, my goal still remained: to choke out any desire in my son to ever do wrong again.

God is merciful. In those two days, He revealed the source of trouble. My Bible study assignment was in Matthew 18:21-35. In the story the king calls for an accounting of all debts. One of his servants, who owed the equivalent of several million dollars, was called in. He couldn't repay the debt. He pleaded, "Lord, have patience and mercy." The king took pity and stamped the servant's account "paid in full."

Later, this same man found another servant who owed him about one day's wages. "Pay up now ... or else," he demanded, with hands clenched around his servant's neck.

The news of this unmerciful man reached the king. He ordered the servant brought before him. "You wicked servant," the king said.

Stunned, I stopped reading. Those words pierced my heart. *Have I been like the wicked servant? Yes, I have.*

To the cross of calvary, I had dragged a weighty bundle of sins, far too large for me to lift. There I had begged Jesus to forgive me. He took pity and lifted the heavy load of sin off my back, thus setting me free. Now in return, I wanted to choke my son for a few injustices. I required of him that which God does not require of me: perfection.

Enlightened, I asked Jesus to forgive me for my lack of mercy. Then I canceled the choke-my-son meeting.

*Lord, thanks for revealing Your precepts in time to save a heartache for our family. Empower me today to be steadfast in obeying Your decrees. Amen.*

Kay David is the author of several devotionals as well as a speaker and a teacher. Besides writing she enjoys reading and raising llamas. Kay and her husband have two children and reside in Greenacres, Washington.

# Look to the Heavens

**Marjorie L. Dodd**

*The heavens declare the glory of God;
the skies proclaim the work of His
hands.* Psalm 19:1, *NIV*

Driving cross-country, I was wrapped in a package of self-pity. I had suffered a betrayal by someone very close to me. Would I ever feel happy or whole again?

In a field to my right, a farmer was plowing under his stunted crop of wheat. A dust cloud almost obliterated my view. The sky held no relief from the months of drought. Just like me, the wheat was dry and without life.

In time, thunderheads appeared on the horizon and gradually billowed higher and higher in the sky. The wind blew. Storm clouds gathered and boiled angrily like the fury within me.

Giant drops spattered on the dusty windshield. First a few, and in minutes a torrent. I stopped to let the shower pass. The parched land drank thirstily. Lightning tore the sky and thunder rolled. I laid my head back and marveled at the power of the storm.

Then the sun broke through, and there against the darkened sky appeared a rainbow. Amid the storm was a glimpse of God's love and promise. Would there be a breakthrough for me?

I opened the car window to the wonderful rush of clean fresh air. The brown earth was renewed and nourished. I got out of the car and stood beside the road. The prairie wheat fields stretched in all directions. The sky, a dome of blue, completely engulfed me. For the first time I began to comprehend the vastness of the universe and felt a small part of this expanse of earth and heavens. The fiery fingers of the sunset streaked across the sky; one minute a blaze of vivid color, the next soft and muted, bringing calm and peace.

As I stopped for the night, the darkness cradled me in its velvet cloak. One by one the stars came out—sparkling pinpoints to reassure me of God's vigil.

In one day, I had witnessed the heavens of power, the reassurance of the rainbow, the glorious majesty of the sunset, and the comfort of night. My God reigns.

*Dear Lord, the heavens show forth Your power, glory, and majesty. Pour out Your tender mercies that heal and nourish me day by day. Amen.*

Marjorie L. Dodd has written a children's book and self-published another. She enjoys oil painting, pen and ink, porcelain art, writing poetry, telling stories, and public speaking. Marjorie and her husband have four children and reside in Bowie, Maryland.

# Innocent Trust

**Mary Jane Donaldson**

*Trust (lean on, rely on and be
confident) in the Lord, and do good;
so shall you dwell in the land and
feed surely on His faithfulness, and
truly you shall be fed.*
Psalm 37:3, *AMP*

The L-1011 soared to 37,000 feet,
over seven miles above the earth, traveling at almost
600 miles per hour. The seat belt sign had been
turned off, and the pilot had greeted all the
passengers and had given us the predicted weather
conditions for our flight; he also told of some points
of interest we would be flying over in the next few
hours.

I looked around observing the different
passengers on the airliner with us. Some were
talking, others were reading or moving about, and
some were being served mixed drinks. I overheard
one passenger say to another, "This drink will make
the flight more bearable."

The other replied, "I have to have a couple before I can even board, then several to hold me until I'm on the ground again."

I looked at my two wide-eyed little granddaughters. One was sitting on my lap, the other on her mother's. They were both satisfied, happy, and content; absolutely no fear was on either of their little faces. Jaoni was asking questions faster than we could answer them, and Paula was sleepily settling down with her thumb and "silky" for the long flight home.

Tears welled up in my eyes as I thought of the unquestioning innocent trust displayed in these children. Not once had they questioned the decisions that now had them up in the clouds far above the earth. They were not afraid. They trusted the ones who loved them; they knew we cared for them and would never hurt them.

I was suddenly overcome with love and emotion as the first verse of Scripture I remember learning as a child came to mind. "Jesus said, 'Let the children come to me and do not hinder them for the kingdom of heaven belongs to such as these'" (Matthew 19:14, *NIV*). Jesus had been speaking of trust in Himself, using children as an example.

The message was clear. Lately, I did not trust Him as these children trusted me. I knew the verse of Scripture in my mind, but I didn't know it experientially in day-to-day living. I was allowing myself to be robbed by humanistic thoughts! Innocent trust had often been stolen by my own reasoning and thought processes, leaving in its place depression, despair, disaster. I realized that kingdom living is reserved for those with childlike trust.

As our plane landed in Los Angeles, I knew God had been speaking to me, trying to teach me a lesson about Himself, as a father would speak to his child. I had gained new insight along with hope and confidence in a heavenly Father who understands His kids.

*Dear Father, please release and deliver me from my own thought patterns and solutions. Once again give me childlike trust to walk in the light of Your Word. And continue to reveal Yourself to me. Amen.*

Mary Jane Donaldson has written several articles, school plays, and devotionals. Formerly a public school assistant teacher, librarian, and writing instructor, she enjoys sewing, reading, walking, cooking, swimming, and clogging. Mary Jane and her husband, John Terrell, have five children and live in Ventura, California.

# For Me, Father?

**Shirley Eaby**

*Good and upright is the Lord:*
*therefore will he teach sinners.*
Psalm 25:8, *KJV*

The sixth-grade girls I taught on
Wednesday evenings at church were live wires, yet
easily bored with the usual "stuff." Singing was one
activity in which I got their cooperation, so we sang
a lot. In each song time I included the chorus, "God
Is So Good." I determined that in spite of themselves
those girls would learn at least one doctrinal
statement about God. Sneaky? Sure, but it was for
their own good. As a result, the words of that little
chorus stuck in my mind, too, and I sang it often.

There was no song in my heart months later as I
sat on a hospital bed, stunned by the word *cancer*—
breast cancer. All the brightness of life was gone in
that moment, snuffed out by that dreaded diagnosis.
I writhed in rising disbelief. I felt tricked—tricked by
my good health, my active life-style, the diagnosis of
my doctors, and most of all by my God.

"I can't believe it, God," I argued. "I don't feel sick. I've had no warning. This can't be happening to me!" Nonacceptance flared, clouding my thinking and dragging me into despair.

Then that "come now, let us reason together" faith fought back:

*Why can't you believe it? You gotta'go sometime and you're prepared to die since you've trusted in Christ Jesus. No warning, huh? The soreness that caused you to find that lump is unusual for the early stages of cancer, isn't it? That sounds like a warning. You're here in the hospital, right? So, it has happened. And, why are you addressing Him with that impersonal God? He's your Father.*

Yes, yes, my Father-God loves me. The gift of his Son proves it. God is so good. Yes, it's just like the chorus says. That chorus hadn't been for the kids! God wants me to learn that truth.

Tears coursed down my cheeks as I sang in that hospital bed, and I sobbed as I ended the chorus with the words, "He's so good to me." Oh, I didn't sing louder than a whisper, but I did sing, believing. That's how I accepted the cancer as something my Father allowed to happen to me.

Fourteen years later I still agree with the Psalmist who wrote, "Thou art good, and doest good; teach me thy statutes" (Psalm 119:68, *KJV*).

*While I live, Father, may I be a witness to Your goodness. Thank You for caring enough to prepare me for the difficulties of this life. Amen.*

Shirley Eaby has had numerous articles published and previously wrote news and features for a weekly newspaper. She is currently registrar for the St. Davids Christian Writers' Conference and enjoys reading, sewing, backpacking, and playing tennis and volleyball. She and her husband have five children and reside in Lancaster, Pennsylvania.

# Filling The Void

**Beverly Eliason**

*Thou madest him to have dominion
over the works of thy hands; thou has
put all things under his feet.*
Psalm 8:6, *KJV*

Because I came to know Jesus while walking in the woods, I learned a reverence for nature that led me into the environmental movement.

There was a stretch of woodland, along a creek, that survived for a while after the land around it was developed. Its peacefulness drew me there day after day. Trees muted nearby traffic noise to a murmur no louder than the hum of insects. Sunbeams filtered through the tree branches in an everchanging play of light and shadow.

God's presence seemed close when I was near trees. It grew closer still when the limbs were bare, but swollen with unborn buds. I felt the promise of eternal life within the dormant wood.

With spring came the bulldozers. The woods disappeared, replaced by a strip of stores crammed full of things no one really needed. Minnows no longer darted through leaf-brown water. The creek died, strangled with litter and silt. Soon, all that remained of nature's abundance were a few dandelions struggling up through cracks in the macadam.

As I mourned the loss of my little woodland, I came to realize that being a Christian means having deep concern for the earth. Jesus lived a life in harmony with nature. I felt His presence in the works of His Father's hand. Surely, when God gave man dominion over the earth, it was a sacred trust.

I've joined in many losing battles since then. In the political arena, economic interests win out over ecological concerns time after time. While I still support public action, I now feel my greatest contribution starts in my own home. With the Lord's help, I can set an example through my own life-style. I can teach my children that happiness has little to do with status symbols and possessions. It is when we lose communion with God that we are driven to a frantic pursuit of anything that might fill up the emptiness in our lives. We pollute our surroundings with the refuse of our momentary satisfactions.

If I can open my children's hearts to God's love, their lives will be too full for the wastefulness and greed that poison our environment.

*Heavenly Father, let my heart be always open to Your love and my life filled with grace. Keep me ever mindful of my sacred trust to care for Your creation. Amen.*

Beverly Eliason has written environmental and newspaper articles as well as numerous devotionals and poems, Sunday School lessons, and stories. In addition, she volunteers counseling with Episcopal Community Services. Beverly is married, has five children, and makes her home in Newtown Square, Pennsylvania.

# Let Not Your Heart Be Troubled

**Marjorie K. Evans**

*Precious in the sight of the Lord is
the death of his saints.*
Psalm 116:15, *KJV*

Troubled thoughts raced through
my mind as I sat beside my mother in her hospital
bed in western Kansas. *How can I leave Mother? I
know I'll probably never see her on earth again; the
doctor has said the cancer is terminal. But I have to
go home; my leave of absence from school is over.*

As I held Mother's hand and once again read to
her from her beloved Bible, I thought of the past ten
days and of how bittersweet they had been.

Even though the cancer had weakened her body,
I felt Mother's spiritual strength, as we talked about
our Lord and Savior, Jesus Christ, and as we
reminisced about days and years of long ago. I knew
I would never forget the love in Mother's brown eyes
and the sweet look of peace on her face when she

said, "Marjorie, whenever my Lord is ready to take me Home, I'm ready to go with Him."

But now it was time for my son Charles, who was on emergency leave from the Air Force, and me to return to California. So it was with heavy hearts that we bade Mother farewell.

As our plane headed in a westerly direction, I was withdrawn and sad. Charles sat quietly beside me understanding my concern and need for introspection.

Suddenly he touched my arm and said softly, "Mom, look up."

I gazed ahead into the most beautiful sunset I had ever seen. Giant splashes of red blending into orange, gold, and yellow were painted across the sky. Huge clouds tinted with rays from the setting sun resembled multi-turreted castles.

Awestruck, I drank in the beauty, and God spoke to my heart. "Marjorie, don't worry about your mother. She is my child and will soon be here to dwell in the mansion I have prepared for her. These heavens are a mere sample of the splendor she'll view when she arrives to spend eternity with me."

Comforted, I recalled, "Let not your heart be troubled: ye believe in God, believe also in me. In my Father's house are many mansions" (John 14:1-2).

*Thank You, dear Heavenly Father, for Your unfathomable love and provision for all Your saints and for giving me a glimpse of Your glory. Amen.*

Marjorie K. Evans is a free-lance writer who enjoys grandmothering, reading, traveling, swimming, and taking care of her plants. In addition, she and her husband, Edgar, are on a ministry team with their church. The Evans have two grown sons and make their home in Downey, California.

# Remember the Blessings

**Betty Steele Everett**

*Praise the Lord, O my soul, and*
*forget not all his benefits.*
Psalm 103:2, *NIV*

A friend had died suddenly in a city hundreds of miles from home. She had gone there for a vacation, apparently in good health, but now she was dead.

As I sat in the church waiting for the funeral service to begin, I was sad and could see no reason to be otherwise. A woman who had served her Lord, her church, and her community was gone. There seemed no cause to praise God for this loss!

Then the woman sitting next to me leaned over to whisper, "We'll miss her so much, but wasn't it wonderful to have known her for so long?"

Immediately I felt both guilt and comfort. I had not stopped to remember the joy and good times God had given me while I knew and worked with this woman for many years. I had not thanked nor praised Him for that. I had thought only of today's loss, not the days of good talk and laughter that we had enjoyed together.

It's easy to forget the good things in our lives. One bad experience seems to wipe them from our memory. Yet David says we are to praise the Lord, and by doing this, we will remember all His benefits to us.

Since that funeral, I have tried to take a few minutes each day to name at least one good thing God has let me enjoy that day. Some days it's easy— a letter from a grandchild printed in big black letters on blue lined paper or a beautiful sunset. Other days it takes me a little longer to name the blessing for the day, but I have never come up empty!

*Help me, Lord, to remember Your benefits, especially during the bad times, because that's when I need to recall Your goodness most of all. Amen.*

Betty Steele Everett has written several books and many articles and has taught at Christian writers' conferences. Betty enjoys traveling, reading, and networking with other Christian writers. She and her husband have two grown children and reside in Defiance, Ohio.

# Mignight Vigil

**Doris Elaine Fell**

*At midnight I rise to give you thanks.*
Psalm 119:62, *NIV*

To me, midnight was the time for sleeping, not for rising. But Mom, ill and frail—a mite of a lady with a spunky spirit—had a built-in alarm clock that went off automatically at the midnight hour. I would tumble and stumble out of bed, my own inner barometer rising rapidly to stormy.

I'd fuss and fume, my frustration mounting. She would smile and say cheerily, "Oh, there's my daughter. Good morning, Doris," or, "I want to get up now and pack for my trip." She would hug me with her smile, and I'd go on fussing and fuming.

In my fury, I would end up in the living room with my Bible, a hymnbook, and tissue, creeping humbly back through the Scriptures to the Lord who never sleeps nor slumbers. To the One who is ever speaking to the Father on our behalf. And it seemed as I read, tissue in hand, that the Lord was saying,

"There's my child. There's Doris."

I'd find reproof, comfort, or challenge, depending on the level of my barometer, spiritual nuggets rising from God's Word into my heart. Sometimes I'd be there for hours learning to say thank you. I'd sing, miserably off-key, and the Lord would send His loving balm as though I had never missed a note.

Then I would go back to Mom's room, sometimes only moments later, other times an hour or more. And she would still be awake, waiting, her hazel eyes following me, her gaze so gentle. I'd sit in the chair beside her bed and hold her hand. Or, if she chose, I'd help her stand so she could walk the length of the mobile home with her walker. I'd give her one of those cups of cold water or juice or hot chocolate in Jesus' name. And we would talk. And always at midnight or in those predawn hours we would sing, she on key.

She would grow weary finally and as I helped her back into bed, we would say the Twenty-third Psalm together—the words *the Lord is my Shepherd* rising like a paean of praise at the midnight hour.

*Father, I thank You that You have no office hours. I thank You that even in the midnight hours of our lives, we may turn to You and offer You our praise— and find You always listening. Amen.*

Doris Elaine Fell is the author of six books and several articles and short stories. She has followed a multifaceted career as a teacher, nurse, missionary, and free-lance writer. Doris makes her home in Huntington Beach, California.

# Footholds for Beauty

**Linda Fischer**

*Remember not the sins of my youth
and my rebellious ways; according to
your love remember me, for you are
good, O Lord.* Psalm 25:7, *NIV*

We had been on the move the past eight years. It felt good to settle in and put down roots.

When the time came to turn my attention to the yard, I found an abundance of large rocks. Frustrated, I could only think how much it would cost to haul in good soil. A thankful heart and a joy for the Lord were gone. My grumbling had allowed the enemy a foothold with my attitude. I sat back and prayed; the idea of a rock garden emerged.

It wasn't hard finding books on rock gardens, but they all looked like plans for *Better Homes and Gardens* magazine. I didn't have the funds for such an elaborate setup. However, I did have plenty of rocks. Seeing the rocks as a good start, I asked the Lord for a plan, one that suited my yard and budget.

With zeal I went to work. I would glow at every opportunity to share what the yard would look like when I was through. I imagined cascading plants filling the crevices, with daisies and asters springing up here and there. As I dug, I no longer became annoyed when I hit another rock.

Then God began to impress upon me how my life was similar to my yard. It looked as if it would take a lot of time and effort to make me into something, but Jesus had a plan. He could use the rocks of divorce, abuse, and heartbreaks in my life, turning them around to make me beautiful in His eyes.

*Dear Lord, let me not forget that You are a God of goodness and love. You can make use of the rocks in my life, turning them into footholds for Your beauty. All I need to do is to trust my life with You. Amen.*

Linda Fischer is a free-lance writer who also enjoys oil painting, needlework, and gardening. She has written several poems and newsletters for a variety of groups. Linda and her husband have two grown sons and make their home in Peshastin, Washington.

# Borrowed Strength

**Marilou H. Flinkman**

*I love you, O Lord, my strength.*
Psalm 18:1, *NIV*

Eight-year-old Mandy burst through the door, bringing bright sunshine with her.

"How was school?" I asked, picking up the papers and lunch box she'd tossed on the table.

"Great! I told teacher you'd bring cupcakes to the open house tonight."

"What?" I cried in dismay.

"I told you last week we have open house tonight at seven." She looked a little guilty. "Didn't I bring the invitation home?"

A cloud covered the sunshine her presence had brought. She looked so innocent, I gave her a hug. "I'll bake cupcakes."

"Can I go to Robin's to play?"

My daughter was gone as quickly as she'd appeared. I glanced at the clock and sighed at the thought of getting cupcakes ready by seven. If I hurried I could get them in the oven before I had to start supper.

"No eggs!" I groaned. I'd been too busy to shop and planned to buy groceries tomorrow. "I'll have to borrow some from Gwen," I muttered, heading out the back door to my neighbors.

"You look tired, Mary. Come have a cup of tea."

"Wish I had time, but Mandy just sprung it on me that I have to bake cupcakes for open house at school tonight. I came begging."

Gwen smiled. "Sorry, I don't have any cupcakes. What else can I help you with?"

"I need to borrow some eggs." I sank down on a kitchen chair. "Wish I could borrow some strength too."

"You can." Gwen sat opposite me. "The Lord is always ready to help. Whenever our cupboard is empty, He's there with whatever we need." My friend put her hand over mine. "Just like the eggs, all you have to do is ask."

When I carried my borrowed eggs home, I didn't feel nearly as harried as when I'd left my kitchen. It was true. In my human frailness, my cup of strength had run dry, but the Lord heard my prayer and filled my cup to the brim.

*O Lord, give me strength to live another day. Help me not to turn cowardly from the difficulties that confront me, but to do my duty with a loving heart. Amen.*

Marilou H. Flinkman has had numerous articles, stories, and devotions published. She enjoys reading, fishing, and white water rafting. Marilou and her husband have six children and reside in Enumclaw, Washington.

# The Great Physician Heals Hearts Too

**Kira L. Flores**

*He heals the broken-hearted and*
*binds up their wounds.*
Psalm 147:3, *NKJV*

A year ago my life was seemingly shattered by the realization that I had been victimized sexually as a child of eleven.

When I became a Christian eleven years ago, I neatly shoved all of my past under the Cross, claiming 2 Corinthians 5:17 as a basis for not dealing any further with what I would later come to know as child abuse.

But our Lord is too gracious to put bandages on our deeply embedded, festering wounds. Through a series of events, He brought me face to face with reality. Although recognizing the truth of what had happened to me explained a lot of the symptoms I'd been suffering from for years, symptoms like depression, anger, food obsession, that recognition also caused intense pain. Therefore, from the beginning of this crisis, the Lord gave me His promise in Psalm 147:3.

I was very confused at that time. There were well-meaning Christians who gave me harmful advice, "You're a new creation; the past is past. You don't need to deal with it." And then as I began attending a support group I heard the following: "Now that you've opened up your past, plan on years, or a lifetime, spent working through the anger and the pain." I didn't want to pretend that my past did not exist, but neither did I wish to spend years or a lifetime in misery!

Despite my confusion, the Lord faithfully led me to a church where I was able to receive compassionate, biblical counseling from my pastor, a victim of abuse himself, now a healed helper. During this counseling, the Lord took me back to each painful event, where He washed me, bound up my wounds, and healed me. Mine was not a case of one event; there were many. Nevertheless, one thousand acts of abuse would not have been too many for my Lord to heal.

Today the abuse of my past no longer carries with it the power to destroy my self-worth, because a greater Power has visited my heart, a greater Power has ministered to my wounds: His name is Jesus!

*Lord Jesus, I thank You for Your healing touch, for Your compassion and Your tenderness. I thank You that when I open up my heart to You, You heal me of my brokenness and bind up all my wounds. Amen.*

Kira L. Flores has been journaling since the age of fourteen. She is a poet and enjoys singing occasionally with her husband who leads worship at their church. The Floreses have two daughters and make their home in El Cajon, California.

# My Portion Forever

**Audrey E. Franson**

*My flesh and my heart may fail, but
God is the strength of my heart and
my portion forever.*
Psalm 73:26, *NASB*

Reality hit me like a sweeping winter chill. The numbness that had become a protective shield began to give way to the truth that, yes, my husband was gone.

He had tried to prepare us. The peace and strength he displayed in the midst of pain and struggle with cancer had been a blessing to so many. He demonstrated a confidence in God's sovereignty and direction, sharing the victory he knew was his in Christ. "I'm a winner either way" became his motto.

That evening, with everyone gone back to their own responsibilities, the grief I'd been trying to hold back poured out in a flood of emotion. I missed Chuck; I wanted him back.

The tape of his message preached one week ago beckoned to me. I carefully placed it in the stereo and sat down, still overwhelmed with the reality of death. I began to listen to the voice that had for so many years been my encouragement and comfort.

My tears subsided. I listened almost as if for the first time to a message of God's strength, His provision and peace in all circumstances of life. Suddenly, shocked back to the present, a peace I can never explain surrounded me. Those tears that had flowed so uncontrollably had washed me freshly in the promise that the Lord will never leave me nor forsake me, and that God's strength, the same strength that carried Chuck these past months, will always be there for me to draw from.

*Lord, thank You for Your presence. May I always remember even in the hard times, that I am not alone. The road ahead may be rough, but, Lord, help me to claim Your promise to be my portion forever. Amen.*

Audrey E. Franson has written programs and plays for her church and enjoys painting, sewing, and handwork. Recently widowed, she is the mother of four children and makes her home in Auburn, Washington.

# God's Symphony

**Mary Francess Froese**

*By them shall the fowls of the heaven*
*have their habitation, which sing*
*among the branches.*
Psalm 104:12, *KJV*

I sit quietly in my perennial garden and enjoy the morning awakening around me. As the first rays of the early morning sun begin to peek over the mountain, I can feel their warmth caress my back. The glitter of the rays causes the dew on the flowers to sparkle like diamonds. Little patches of fog linger in the canyon below, creating an unearthly aura. There is such a quietness that even the sound of breathing seems an intrusion.

Then, as the top of the sun bursts over the ridge of the mountain, the birds begin their morning song. What a symphony! Never have I been so in tune to the sights and sounds of the morning. I sit spellbound. The cool air is filled with beautiful music. Each bird seems to sing a different melody, but the blend is exquisite.

After awhile, I notice that one of the birds has a very monotonous trill—over and over the same few notes burst forth into the air. Suddenly this same bird stops singing. Immediately I sense a real loss in the total symphony. The void of this one little trill makes such a difference. After a few moments he rejoins the others, renewed and strong, and the symphony is whole again.

I smile, for in that little scenario I sense my Father speaking to my spirit. "Those little birds are precious to Me; they give Me great pleasure. How much more are you to Me. You may think yourself ordinary, or insignificant, but you are very important in My symphony of life. You are the only you I created. Were it not for you there would be a real void in My world. So live and remember you are very valuable to Me."

*Father, Your love is shown in such wondrous ways. Thank You for opening my eyes and ears to Your magnificent love that surrounds me. Amen.*

Mary Francess Froese is a free-lance writer who contibutes to several magazines and inspirational publications. Her first book, *Heroes of a Special Kind*, was released in 1991 by Evergreen. Mary and her husband, Allen, have two grown sons and make their home in Vista, California.

# Please Hurry!

**Mona Gansberg-Hodgson**

*Wait for the Lord; Be strong, and let
your heart take courage; Yes, wait for
the Lord.* Psalm 27:14, *NASB*

**M**y mom gave me a special
Mother's Day gift one year when my daughters were
small. It wasn't an elaborate gift, only a simple mug.
And yet it was full of understanding and recognition.

On the front of the mug stood a frazzled woman.
Her hair hung stringy, her tattered clothes drooped,
and mischievous children clamored at her feet.
Under the bewildered mother was this prayer:
"Grant me patience, Lord, but please hurry!"

I laughed in recognition of that woman on the
mug; I had seen her in the mirror just the day
before. And she could definitely use more patience.
The mug was funny, but the prayer on it hit home.

Our society feeds on impatience. We have instant
coffee, instant credit, instant winners, instant rice,
and instant replays. There are drive-up windows at
banks, dry cleaners, fast-food restaurants, and

convenience stores. We rush to the shortest line at the market, and we are angered by motorists who slow us down.

Even my prayers are fueled by impatience. I find myself wanting to rush God. Sometimes His replies don't come quick enough for me. Or maybe in my hurry, I'm not listening for His answer.

Yes, God has promised to hear our prayers and to answer our calls. But, He didn't promise instant results. Instead, we are told to "wait for the Lord." In His perfect time, He will answer.

*Father God, I am grateful that You are the Father of time. Help me to be patient and to seek Your perfect timing in all things. Amen.*

Mona Gansberg-Hodgson has had numerous articles, poems, and devotionals published. In addition to being a writer and speaker, Mona enjoys hiking, camping, writing letters, and traveling. She and her husband, Bob, have two daughters and reside in Cottonwood, Arizona.

# A Refuge in a Storm

**Martha E. Garrett**

*But as for me, I shall sing of Thy
strength; Yes, I shall joyfully sing of
Thy lovingkindness in the morning.
For Thou hast been my stronghold,
And a refuge in the day of my
distress. Psalm 59:16, NASB*

Don't worry, Paul," I said to my
husband. "No matter what happens, things will work
out all right." In my heart I wasn't convinced, but I
hoped to lift some of the burden of grief from him.
Because of leukemia, which was devastating his
body, he was filled with concern for our family's
future.

Before my husband's illness, life had seemed so
secure. Then suddenly with his death everything
changed. Our family became uprooted. We sold our
home and headed to the West Coast.

One day, still a thousand miles from our new
home in California where my brother lived, my four
children and I sat at the counter of an almost

deserted cafe in Nevada, waiting patiently for breakfast.

The door of the cafe opened, and a young couple with their child walked directly to the counter and sat beside us. Almost immediately the woman started talking about a wonderful Bible study in their hometown. Although I had been active in a prestigious church and had taught a Sunday School class for years, I knew almost nothing about the Bible. Suddenly I had a great longing to be part of a Bible study group.

"Where is your hometown?" I inquired.

"It's a town in California about a thousand miles from here," my new friend answered. I gasped in amazement when she told me the name of the town. That was *our* destination; the location of our new home; a new way of life.

True to the promise in Scripture, God did provide for us new hope and a new future through the Bible study which we had learned about in Nevada. We found that our security was not in circumstances or location but in the reality of Jesus Christ, a reality we discovered when we centered our lives around the Word of God.

*Thank You, Lord, for guiding us into Your Word. Thank You for being our strength, our stronghold, our refuge. Amen.*

Martha E. Garrett is a published writer who also enjoys reading, letter writing, traveling, manuscript critiquing, encouraging writers, and being with friends. She has two sons and two daughters and makes her home in East Wenatchee, Washington.

# *He Is My Comfort When Tears Flow*

**Denise George**

*May your unfailing love be my comfort.* Psalm 119:76, *NIV*

I remember the hot August day I sat in the yellow porch swing grieving the death of my beloved grandmother. Expecting my second child within a few days, I couldn't travel to the funeral some three hundred miles away. I was alone that weekend except for the company of my two-year-old son to comfort me.

"Why, God?" I asked again and again. "Why did you allow my grandmother to die before my daughter, her only namesake, was born?" How I wanted her to be able to cuddle my new infant at least one time.

Death in the midst of new life. I wondered how I could concentrate on the life brimming inside of me when I was so overcome by the death all around me.

My small son, Christian, saw my tears. I tried to explain my deep grief to a child I thought too young to understand. Big blue eyes in a tiny face surrounded by a mop of tousled blond hair stared at me in puzzlement. Then Christian did something unexpected. Lovingly, he encircled my face with his chubby little hands and spoke the words my grandmother had so often spoken to me: "It'll be all right," he said and then smiled.

And, somehow, upon hearing those familiar words, I knew that it really would be all right—that God was close beside me, comforting me in the death of my grandmother and in the upcoming birth of my daughter.

For the rest of the weekend, I sat in the porch swing rocking gently and thanking God for the gift of comfort He had sent to me in the form of a little child.

*Oh, Lord, You are so close, even when life seems confusing, even when tears flow. Thank You for Your love, for the comfort You send to me through others. Amen.*

Denise George has written nine books and numerous articles and is a frequent speaker for writers' conferences and women's retreats. Denise and her husband have a son and a daughter and make their home in Birmingham, Alabama.

# A Goodly Heritage

**Donna Clark Goodrich**

*The lines are fallen unto me in
pleasant places; yea, I have a goodly
heritage.* Psalm 16:6, *KJV*

One of my earliest recollections is
of my mother getting us four children ready every
Sunday morning and walking with us over a mile to
the bus stop to go to church.

Later, when we moved into town, our house was
the gathering place for all the neighborhood children.
We sang around the piano, put jigsaw puzzles
together, and answered questions out of a quiz book.
At the end of the evening, my mother made cocoa or
popcorn. In years to come, she became "Mom" to
many of our friends who felt free to come and talk
with her about their problems.

I remember when we sold that home, she bought
my brothers the horns they wanted and I received an
accordion. It was Mother's dream that her children
would be musical. She took in ironing to pay my
brothers' five-dollar band fee each semester.

My mother was a woman of prayer. One night we needed food and she prayed. In less than an hour, a friend brought by some money she had owed my mother for several years. It had "come to her mind" that evening. She was going to bring it by the next day, but something urged her, "No, take it tonight," and she arrived before the grocery store closed.

Mother encouraged me to date only Christian boys, and many times I returned from a date to find her asleep on her knees.

It wasn't long before the family circle grew smaller. The three older children married and I moved to another state. There I met a seminary student and became engaged.

On my wedding day, as Mother helped me into my long white gown, she expressed disappointment that she could not buy me an expensive wedding gift. But I told her then, and many times afterward, that she had given me the finest wedding gift a daughter could ask for—the heritage of a Christian mother!

*Lord, help me, through my words and my example, to leave my children the same kind of heritage my mother left me. Amen.*

Donna Clark Goodrich has published several books, short stories, and articles. She organized and leads two Christian writers' clubs, teaches at writers' seminars across the country, and founded the yearly Arizona Christian Writers' Conference. Donna and her husband have three grown children and live in Mesa, Arizona.

# The Sleep Connection

**Marjorie Gordon**

*In peace I will both lie down and sleep; for thou alone, O Lord, makest me dwell in safety.* Psalm 4:8, *RSV*

White hospital sheets felt crisp and cold against my skin. Outside the sky grew dark; storm clouds ushered in the night.

Thoughts of tomorrow's surgery increased my anxiety. I'm a registered nurse so I can worry about risks and complications most people don't suspect. The tumor—malignant or benign? The anesthesia—sometimes it can have devastating if not fatal effects.

I opened my Bible and prayed. "Lord, I know Your promise that You will never leave me nor forsake me. Encourage me now especially for what awaits me."

I decided to read in the book of Psalms—always something worth meditating about there. I stopped suddenly after reading Psalms 4:8. The words leaped off the page and tackled the turmoil within. "In peace I will both lie down and sleep; for thou alone,

O Lord, makest me dwell in safety."

I read the passage over and over. Then I copied it onto a slip of paper to keep nearby. The matter was settled. I slept in wonderful peace.

In the morning when the attendant arrived to cart me off to surgery, I quickly read the promise once again. I knew God would make me sleep safely, even under the anesthesia.

This chapter of my life had begun in a dark valley, but it had led to an exhilarating mountaintop. When a new roommate arrived the evening following my surgery, I sensed devastation was her companion. She faced the same surgery I had experienced. With confidence and joy I shared my treasure from Psalm 4 with her. She was equally comforted and sustained.

We later learned we were the talk of the staff on our surgical ward. Nurses actually felt our contagious peace whenever they entered our room.

*Lord, thank You for watching over me with such tender care, and for giving me just the right words of assurance at exactly the right time. It's so comforting to know nothing is too large or too small for Your concern. Amen.*

Marjorie Gordon has been published in several magazines and is a Bible study leader and speaker for women's groups. She enjoys reading and painting and is currently working as a registered nurse. Marjorie and her husband have three grown children and reside in Vancouver, Washington.

# Renewed Hope

**Bonnie S. Grau**

*Wait on the Lord: be of good courage,*
*and he shall strengthen thine heart:*
*wait, I say, on the Lord.*
Psalm 27:14, *KJV*

I was hurt and disappointed by
someone who didn't seem to have time for me
anymore. Our relationship had deteriorated and that
troubled me. I wanted things to be right between us.

It was a Saturday morning and I had planned to
sleep a little later than usual. But I awoke early
with the words of our last conversation ringing in my
ears.

"If I had time I'd talk to you, but I don't have
time," she had said.

I slipped out of bed, made myself a cup of coffee,
and went to my quiet corner. The last few weeks had
been busy ones and I had not been spending much
time there.

For a while, I enjoyed the comfort of God's Word
and the fellowship of prayer. Then I saw the parallel.

How I must hurt my heavenly Father when I don't have time—when my devotions are hurried and my conversations with Him take place as I'm running here and there.

I began to squirm under the scrutiny of my thoughts. I saw how unbalanced I had become. And I confessed, with shame, my neglect.

That's when I recognized the greater implications. I saw that just as my Father is willing to wait for me, I need to be patient through the stages of human relationships. Sometimes I even need to step aside while He works in the lives of others.

But as my Father continues to care for me when I am distant, should I not continue to show love and concern when relationships are strained?

I know that this will not be easy for my impatient nature. However, once again, my quiet time has brought me hope and direction. Because of that, I can trust God to heal the hurts. I'm now willing to wait until there's time to talk.

*Father, thank You for the lessons You're ready to teach when I'm ready to listen. Help me to be obedient to the instructions You give. Amen.*

Bonnie S. Grau besides writing enjoys reading, traveling, music, and being active in women's ministries. She is also a substitute teacher and writes feature articles for her local newspaper. She and her husband have two daughters and make their home in Marysville, Pennsylvania.

# Darkness Turned Into Light

**Carol Green**

*You, O Lord, keep my lamp burning;
my God turns my darkness into light.
With your help I can advance against
a troop; with my God I can scale a
wall.* Psalm 18:28, *NIV*

**M**y mobility instructor guided me by the arm to the long driveway in front of my house. "A perfect place to practice," she said.

Darkness pressed in all around me while familiar and unfamiliar sounds poked into the warmth of that afternoon. Click, click, click. *What was that?* I thought. My instructor placed into my right hand the white cane she had just clicked open. As she positioned my fingers in the golf grip, she said, "Hold it stiff-armed, centered in front of you. Then tap right and step with your left foot. Tap left and step with your right foot."

As she spoke she gently moved my cane first

right, then left. My body followed her leading, but my mind taunted, *Now everyone will know you are blind. You can't hide it by hanging onto the arm of your husband. People will stare and pity you.* I shook my head to rid myself of these thoughts.

I tapped left and stepped right. Feeling like an ugly duckling, I waddled down the driveway. I tapped right and stepped left. "Good, good," my instructor said. I turned and started up the driveway. "Stop. You're out of step. Start again."

Tap left. Step right. My back, shoulder, and arm muscles ached. I remembered the words of Psalm 18: "God turns my darkness into light." The words didn't take away the stiffness or my uncertainty, but they did give me the courage not to quit.

Scrape, clink! *What was that? A wall?* No, the garage door. Again I remembered the words of the Psalm. I smiled and shared them with my instructor. "With my God I can scale a wall." We both laughed and some of the tenseness left me.

Today, I still struggle and use my white cane with much uncertainty, afraid of scrapes and falls. But God keeps my lamp burning, turning my darkness into light.

*Dear Lord, be with those today who struggle with visible and invisible handicaps. Turn their darkness of fear, anger, depression, or uncertainty into light, the light of Your love. Thank You for walking with me no matter where my path leads. Amen.*

Carol Green, in addition to writing, enjoys artwork and exhibits, theater and concerts. She is a co-leader of a Bible study group and plans women's retreats. Carol and her husband, Richard, have three grown children and reside in Walnut Creek, California.

# Surprise!

**Carlene Hacker**

*Behold, children are a gift of the
Lord.* Psalm 127:3, *NASB*

PREGNANT!" I gasped to my
doctor, "I'm too old! I can't be!" But I was—on both
counts.

"Children are a gift of the Lord," I read. But I
already had two gifts: a nine-year-old daughter and
an eleven-year-old son. Now that they were in school,
it was time for me to read romance novels and plant
a garden and enroll in an art class. Instead, I bought
a book of names for the baby, and my delighted
husband and I joined a Lamaze class.

I cried a lot. Everyone told me that being
emotional was part of being pregnant; I agreed. They
said my face was glowing; all I saw was my stomach
growing. I was ashamed of my feelings and tried to
feel grateful and blessed. But most of the time I felt
old and tired, so I dyed my graying hair.

When I began to feel life, God began to soften my
heart. A baby, not an accumulation of cells, but a
live baby was growing inside of me! My doctor asked
if he could do an amniocentesis, which reveals any

abnormalities before birth. "Because of your age, you know." I knew, but refused, telling the doctor what I believed—that life is sacred and God-given. No test results could change that. But God used that to change me, and finally I accepted my pregnancy and asked God to forgive my selfishness.

However, I did want a girl. (My daughter wanted a Saint Bernard!) Yet almost one month after my fortieth birthday, my son was born. The moment I saw him, I knew that David Jonathan was a beloved gift of the Lord.

Ten years have now passed, filled with Eskimo kisses, cozy reading times, hockey practices, and all of David's love. "What would I do without you, David?" I ask him. Neither of us knows.

But I'm still dyeing my hair!

*Lord God, only You know what I need. Thank You for being patient and for giving me time to see that Your gifts are good. Amen.*

Carlene Hacker is a published writer who also enjoys gardening and playing the flute and handbells. In addition, she is a board member of the San Diego Christian Writers' Guild. Carlene and her husband, Alan, have three children and reside in El Cajon, California.

# Consider the Moon!

**April Hamelink**

*When I consider Thy heavens, the*
*work of Thy fingers, the moon and the*
*stars, which Thou hast ordained;*
*What is man, that Thou dost take*
*thought of him? And the son of man,*
*that Thou dost care for him?*
Psalm 8:3-4, *NASB*

Hannah knows the moon.
Tonight as we drove home from Grandma's house,
she sat, sleepy and very quiet. Suddenly she pulled
her fingers out of her mouth, sat up straight, and
asked, "Mommy, what's that?"

Above us, bright in the clear summer night was a
harvest moon, white and round and nearly full.
"That's the moon," I answered. "Oh." She sat back,
fingers back in her mouth, eyes transfixed on the
lovely guardian of the night.

Hannah is nearly three years old. We have read
over and over the storybook *Goodnight Moon*. She
has heard on many occasions and in many settings
the Genesis account of when God created the sun to
rule the day and the moon to rule the night. We have
often thanked Jesus for making the beautiful moon
and stars. But tonight, for the very first time, she

127

really knows the moon. Tonight, she experienced the moon.

We have talked about it, read about it, even prayed about it, but tonight the moon became real to her. It is amazing to me that we had driven under a night sky a hundred or more times in her little life and had never pointed out the moon in a way that made it real to her. She had to experience it for herself.

It will be the same for her when she experiences Jesus for the first time. We have read the Bible stories of Jesus, talked about how He interacts in our lives, worshipped Him and prayed to Him. But someday, something will happen in her life that will make her sit up and say, "Mom, what was that?"

And I will answer, "That's Jesus, loving you, asking to be part of your life." A look of wonder will cross her face as she experiences Jesus for the first time. I will be amazed that in her whole life I had never explained Jesus in a way that was real to her. I will praise Him that He cares for her, and that she has experienced Him for herself, and I will pray that she never takes her eyes off the Guardian of her soul.

*Lord, as I consider the moon and the work of Your hands, I am amazed at the depths of Your love. Help me to continue to experience You in my life in new and amazing ways. Amen.*

April Hamelink, in addition to writing, enjoys reading, collecting children's books, teaching Sunday School, and children's ministries. She and her husband, Pete, have three children and make their home in N. Bonneville, Washington.

# Trusting a Faithful God

**Donna Hamilton**

*And he sent a man before them—*
*Joseph, sold as a slave. They bruised*
*his feet with shackles, his neck was*
*put in irons ... till the word of the*
*Lord proved him true.*
Psalm 105:17-19, *NIV*

I first heard it through the grapevine—there were going to be changes affecting the two departments for which I was clerk. Finally it was confirmed; my supervisor was being replaced by a manager from the "front" of the plant. He would be my new boss. Also, he would be heading up seven departments, and I would be responsible for the paperwork of them all.

I was terrified. This manager had a reputation of being tough, exact, and demanding. His former secretary had been with him six years; now he was inheriting me with his new departments. How would we get along? Would I be able to please him? The thought came that perhaps I could transfer to another department, but I liked the job where I was.

As I prayed about my situation, I kept remembering Joseph and the outcome of his life; how God had promoted him after all his trials. Joseph's faithfulness and trust in God through adversity had often encouraged me to hang in there in circumstances I didn't understand. Could God be behind this change and have a plan in it that I could not yet see?

So, with prayers for God's help and His promise of all things working together for good (Romans 8:28), I prepared myself to accept this demanding new boss. And it turned out to be one of the best things that had ever happened to me.

Yes, he was demanding and exact, but he was also appreciative and fair. As I learned to handle new responsibilities, he entrusted me with more, and repaid me with promotion and salary increases. How I thanked God for holding me there in spite of my fears!

This experience and others are teaching me to trust God, no matter what the circumstances. Though sometimes it's hard, and the results or rewards are not quickly seen, I'm learning that in God's own time He will bring good out of the very things that are most difficult.

*O Father, it is good to trust You, to know You never toy with my emotions but have a plan that You are lovingly working out for my good. Amen.*

Donna Hamilton although new to the writing profession has written poems, articles, and devotions. Her hobbies include reading and cooking, and she enjoys studying and teaching God's Word. Donna and her husband, Ed, have five children and make their home in Chino, California.

# The Carpenter and Mrs. "Sew-N-Sew"

**Dena Hamlin**

*Since my youth, O God, you have
taught me, and to this day I declare
your marvelous deeds. Even when I
am old and gray, do not forsake me,
O God, till I declare your power to the
next generation, your might to all
who are to come.*
Psalm 71:17-18, *NIV*

I had sewn for twenty years when
I became the seamstress and counterperson for a dry
cleaners, but I was ill-prepared for some of our
customers' requests.

One day a woman and her teenage son presented
me with a pair of nylon parachute pants. Pointing to

a hole the size of a quarter he asked, "Can you fix it without it showing?"

*Surely you jest*, I thought, but replied, "I'll do what I can."

Seated at the sewing machine, I stared at this ridiculous problem. Naturally I prayed. "Jesus, since You were a carpenter, sewing ought to be no big deal for You. What can I do?" Nothing miraculous came to mind so I ironed a patch on both sides, zigzagged the edges and set the pants aside.

Later that day a wonderful idea fell out of heaven and hit me on the head. I fashioned a pocket of similar fabric like the one on the other side and sewed it over the patched hole. As requested, I had fixed it without it showing!

The Lord further amazed me by sending people to make my job at the dry cleaners easier. For example, one time I needed to replace a jeans zipper but didn't know how. So I slipped the jeans into the bag of extra mending my boss sent out. When he picked up the order, the zipper was only half put in, the second part ready and pinned. He told the lady I'd finish the job. Carefully surveying her work, I learned how the professionals do it.

Later, God gave me invaluable advice from two men. A sewing machine salesman for a quarter of a century showed me how to reduce bulk while hemming jeans. Another man found me pondering how to replace a pair of new pockets in a coat. He said he never completely removed two items at the same time. A mechanic, he always left one brake intact while he replaced the other. That tip came in mighty handy when I had to lengthen the sleeves of a sports jacket for the first time.

With Jesus, the carpenter from Galilee as my chief consultant, I could confidently post this notice:

The difficult we do immediately,
The impossible takes longer,
Miracles by request only!!!

*Thank You Lord, that You have an answer for every single need I face. Truly every gift from You is a marvelous deed! Please give me opportunities to share with others the good ideas You give me. Amen.*

Dena Hamlin, in addition to writing, enjoys cross-stitch and collecting clothing, accessories, and memorabilia from the 1940s. She also collects and makes scale dollhouse miniatures. Dena has three daughters and makes her home in Seattle, Washington.

# *Finkle, Finkle, Liddy Dar*

**Teresa Harbert**

*Even before there is a word on my tongue, Behold, O Lord, Thou dost know it all.* Psalm 139:4, *NASB*

The other day my husband, Dave, and I were driving home from a shopping trip with the kids. As we traveled, our three preschool boys kept busy by chattering among themselves. During a lull in the normal clamor of childish voices and laughter, a single small voice piped up from the backseat:

"Finkle, finkle, liddy dar ...."

Aaron, our two-year-old, was singing joyfully all by himself. Dave and I hadn't realized he knew how to sing. We were amazed as we listened. To anyone else this tuneless little mumble of words would have meant nothing, but to us it was perfectly clear. Our little boy was making his debut as a soloist. Dave

134

and I exchanged proud glances as Aaron's version of "Twinkle, Twinkle, Little Star" filled our car. Smiling to myself, I tucked away another precious memory to savor in the years to come.

It always surprises me when other people can't understand my little one's speech. I guess I am with my children so much of the time that their gibberish makes perfect sense to me. It must be just like that between God and us too. I believe God can understand us just as we understand our own kids.

Sometimes when I pray, I just can't find a way to express what I mean. I struggle to form words for all the feelings churning inside. I'm so glad that no matter how jumbled those thoughts are, God understands me. His desire is to commune with me and He will always honor even my most fumbled attempts. Isn't that incredible? Our perfect and loving Father knows exactly what we mean to say, before we can even find the words to tell Him.

*Lord, help me always to reach up to You in prayer. I'm so thankful You don't need my prayers perfectly polished. You understand me as only a loving parent can understand His own child. Amen.*

Teresa Harbert is a published writer and stay-at-home mom who enjoys gardening, bread making, aerobics, and cross-stitch. She and her husband, Dave, have three sons and make their home in Orangevale, California.

# Transformation

**Dorothy M. Harpster**

*Your word is a lamp to my feet and a*
*light for my path.*
Psalm 119:105, *NIV*

**N**o sunbeams pierced the heavy
cloud cover as I waited for the plane that would fly
me across the country. Rain seemed imminent. The
gloomy day didn't help ease my anxiety and
uncertainty about the decision I'd need to make at
my journey's end.

After some delay, my carrier took off. There was
the rapidly accelerating ride on the runway, the
lifting from the ground, and the climbing into the
atmosphere.

The clouds floating by my window were not dingy
and gray as I'd perceived them from below, but pure
and bright. I longed to reach out to see if they were
as soft as they looked. As we continued upward, we
were soon looking down on the sea of large and small
snow-white, cottony puffs.

It was the sun's light that changed what had
appeared drab into airy, breathtaking beauty, and I
marveled that it is God's creation, the sun, that has

this power to illuminate and make clear. It occurred to me that God is in the transforming business. He can make us into beautiful women if we'll allow Him to lead us. He will give us graceful, loving spirits to enable us to reach out to others and tenderly lift them up.

I thought of that greater light, Jesus, who called Himself the Light of the world. He is the source of wisdom and truth. He can show us which roads to take throughout our lives. And I can communicate with Him any time, any place, and seek His guidance.

Why hadn't I remembered to talk to Him about the burden I'd brought with me? I consciously resolved to no longer fret and worry about it, but to trust in Him.

I smiled as I took my Bible from my carry-on and began to read. My problem wasn't resolved yet, but with God's help I knew it would be. There was no longer room in my heart for anxiety, gloom, and heaviness, for happiness was there.

*Dear Lord, please make me the kind of person You want me to be. Help me to be faithful in searching Your Word daily and applying it to my life. Amen.*

Dorothy M. Harpster is a retired elementary school teacher who enjoys writing, collecting books, and working with youth. Dorothy makes her home in Lewisburg, Pennsylvania.

# A Dance Lesson Down Aisle D

**Pat Hartmann**

*You have turned my mourning into dancing for me; You have put off my sackcloth and girded me with gladness.* Psalm 30:11, *AMP*

I was in a hurry, as usual, racing my shopping cart down the crowded supermarket aisles. I glanced nervously at my watch as I grabbed dinner items from the shelves. I just had time to cruise past the dairy section, stand in the checkout line, and drive home, timing my arrival with that of the school bus and my young son David.

A complaining wheel on the shopping cart squeaked out a rapid tempo as I zoomed to the end of the aisle ready to make a sharp left toward the dairy section. I lurched to a sudden stop as a little old lady started to step out in front of me at the crossroads of canned meats and cheeses. Focusing on her smiling face, I was startled and then delighted when she picked up the edges of her skirt and did a little jig, grinning mischievously as she waved me on. Surprised out of my hurry-up syndrome, I found myself laughing out loud at the spunk and love of life in that lovely woman.

That little jig danced in my mind as I put away groceries at home, smiling at the memory.

"Can we play a game, Mommy?" asked David as he burst enthusiastically through the door. I should have started dinner, of course, and there was that laundry in the dryer. But then life is short, and little boys don't stay little for long. We have to dance our jigs while we can.

I stopped to give my little guy a hug. "Sure, Honey, let's play!"

*Dear Lord, thank You for slowing me down from the busyness of life to see clearly the real business of life. Help me to never be too busy to love my family or those You send my way. Give me Your eyes to see what is really urgent, Your heart to feel peace and hope, and Your dance of true joy!*
*Amen.*

Pat Hartmann is a former teacher and editor and writer of a Christian newspaper. Besides writing, she enjoys painting, wood-carving, and, with her husband, operating a Christmas tree farm. The Hartmanns have eight children and make their home in Ojai, California.

# *Especially in My Own Home*

**Helen Heavirland**

*I will try to walk a blameless path,
but how I need your help, especially
in my own home, where I long to act
as I should.* Psalm 101:2, *TLB*

Can't you let me have a moment's peace?" I growled.

Surprise crossed my husband's face. He turned and left the room.

What had I just said? I wanted so much to be a good witness to him, a new Christian. And yet I sometimes acted in ways that denied God's goodness. Though I studied my Bible and prayed regularly and ministered to others, I was failing in my important mission—my own home.

Distraught, I fell on my knees and laid my heart bare before God. I opened my Bible expecting spiritual answers, but God surprised me.

God reminded me that my body is the temple of the Holy Ghost (1 Corinthians 6:19, *KJV*). I'd be upset if one week when I went to church the sanctuary was full of trash. But did I trash the temple of the Holy Ghost? God laid on my heart that I had been neglecting my body—His temple. He impressed upon me that by taking care of my body I would do more than lengthen life, I would improve my spiritual experience and witness.

I began to squeeze a little exercise—usually a walk—somewhere into most days. I breathed fresh air deeply. I watched my diet more carefully. I said no to things that would overcommit me and steal sleep.

Before long both my family and I marveled at the change. I smiled more. I laughed more easily. I worked efficiently. And I didn't just plop when I stopped. I relaxed. Patience replaced gritted teeth. Energy and enthusiasm dispelled doldrums.

Years later I learned the science that supported the change. But before I understood the science, I knew God's Word was right. My body is His temple. When I take care of my body, I feel better. My brain comprehends the messages of his Word more clearly. I respond more easily to His urgings and to other people's requests.

A healthy apple tree produces apples. A healthy body, the temple of the Holy Ghost, more readily produces His fruit—love, joy, peace, patience, kindness, goodness, faithfulness, gentleness, and self-control (Galatians 5:22,23, *TLB*). When my body is at its best, God can live out His love through me in ways my unfit body would not allow—especially in my most important mission, my own home.

*Creator God, thank You for the marvelous creation of*

*the human body. Help me to care for my body as Your temple so that You can use me more effectively, especially in my own home. Amen.*

Helen Heavirland has written several articles and poems as well as a children's story. She enjoys observing nature, hiking, cross-country skiing, and reading. In addition, she writes music and is a Bible speaker. Helen and her husband, LeRoy, make their home in Kalispell, Montana.

# Faith Journey

## Joy Anne Held

*I will instruct you and teach you in
the way you should go; I will counsel
you and watch over you.*
Psalm 32:8, *NIV*

Resign from your job." The
message invaded my thoughts one evening after a
particularly long day at work.

"That's insane," I said. "I have nothing lined up
anywhere else. How could I live?" Though I had
longed for a change, I dismissed the idea and went
about my business.

"Resign from your job." The message broke
through again, this time clearer than before.

"You can't be serious, God. Where would I go?" I
argued.

"Resign from your job." It weighed heavy on my
heart. *Perhaps He means for me to start looking for
another job, then resign*, I reasoned.

"No. I want you to give your resignation this
week."

This week! My heart jumped into my throat. Maybe I was hearing things. Surely, God wouldn't have me do something so risky. How could I know it was really Him?

As I wrestled with my thoughts, I was reminded that I had asked God to help me grow in the area of faith. Here was my opportunity—what better way to learn than to trust Him so implicitly? But did it have to be so scary?

"All right," I said finally. "I'll do it. While I don't understand what You are doing, or how You'll work it out, I'll resign." As I stilled my trembling heart before God, He instructed me further: Because it would take time for my department to find a replacement editor, and because I was committed to stay in my brother's trailer until he returned from sea duty in late March, I was to give a three-month notice.

My heart was wrapped in both fear and excitement when I gave my resignation that Thursday. Was this how Abraham felt when God gave him his marching orders? I wondered what God had planned for me.

Over the following months, God opened doors I had never dreamed possible. My "promised land" turned out to be a position with a Christian publishing company. God had granted me the desires of my heart—an opportunity to grow as a writer and editor while helping to spread the gospel. What I would have missed if I had allowed fear to keep me from obeying God's voice!

How comforting it is to know that I don't have to have all of the puzzle pieces to step out in faith. While the destination may be unknown to me, it is not unknown to God. I must release God to do what He wants to do in my life. My responsibility is only to do what God has asked me to do and let Him work out His plan in His way and in His time.

*Father, teach me to trust even when I can't understand what You are doing. Help me to remember that because You love me I don't have to be afraid of Your hand. Amen.*

Joy Anne Held is a free-lance writer who enjoys singing, traveling, camping, fishing, hiking, sewing, puppetry, and acting. She has worked as a newspaper reporter and as associate editor for the Salvation Army publication the *New Frontier*. Joy and her husband, Joe, make their home in Santa Barbara, California.

# A Mother's Influence

**Terry Helwig**

*For the Lord is good; his mercy is everlasting; and his truth endureth to all generations.* Psalm 11:5, *KJV*

I was up and down most of the night with my daughter Mandy. She couldn't sleep. Her forehead felt like warm, baked bread and she had that glassy-eyed look that came when she wasn't feeling well. Finally, I asked, "Would you like to sleep in the guest room with me?"

She nodded and her padded footsteps followed me into the bedroom. During the next several hours, I fluffed her pillow, held a cold washcloth against her forehead, and stroked the wisps of hair around her face. I heard the hallway clock dong five times. At that hour, motherhood seemed a thankless, tiring job. I was sure that Mandy, in the passing years, would not even remember this night of fever and lost sleep.

Then, as if on cue, I felt a warm hand cup my neck. Mandy drew me close, patted me, and whispered something that would probably never have been spoken had she been feeling well. She said, "I can't believe I'm going to be this kind to my child someday."

Her words awakened something within me. For the first time, I was struck with the awesome responsibility that God has given us mothers. How we treat our children, what we teach them, the fragile blooms of faith we hand them, and many patterns for living and loving will be passed on to our grandchildren and the generations after them.

As I thought of my daughter tenderly caring for my grandchild, a smile came over my weary face. I drew the cool washcloth across her brow and kissed her. Motherhood was not a thankless job—especially if the tenderness could be passed from one generation to the next.

Even though Mandy might not recall that night, perhaps she would carry forth the love that filled it. With that thought, I too drifted off to sleep ... still holding a wet washcloth and my daughter's hand.

*Dear Father, help me to understand that while the memory of days may fade, the love that fills them is not easily forgotten. Amen.*

Terry Helwig is the author of two books and numerous magazine articles and is a contributor to *Daily Guideposts*. She enjoys nature walks, traveling, reading, and photography. Terry and her husband, Jim, have one daughter and reside in Englewood, Colorado.

# A Better Gift!

**Carolyn Henderson**

*You have made known to me the path
of life; you will fill me with joy in
your presence, with eternal pleasures
at your right hand.* Psalm 16:11, *NIV*

**M**y most vivid childhood
memories, memories that I can almost smell and see,
are those of wanting to become an artist. I loved to
color with crayons, draw with chalk, and finger
paint! I could feel myself standing taller every time
someone said that I had a real gift for art. I just
knew I wanted to become an artist.

The year I graduated from high school, I also got
married. We had our first baby shortly after our first
anniversary, then a second daughter two years later.
And soon after I began to wonder, *Will I ever have
time for myself?* It wasn't that I didn't love my
husband and children, but it seemed that I was
always giving and never receiving. The idea of
developing my gift for art seemed far from reality.

When my second daughter was out of diapers, I

thought finally the time had come for me to go back to school. I couldn't wait! Every evening, after the girls were safely asleep, I'd pour over the college class schedule. What class would I take first? It was fun just to think of the possibilities.

But before registration at the college started, I found that I was pregnant again. And I began thinking, Wasn't I living in a time when a woman had a choice? A right over her own body? My mind whirled like the laundry that was spinning in the dryer. How would I ever have the financial ability to go back to school now? Or the energy? I was already too tired. And what about time? Caring for the girls took up most of my time.

I filled the next weeks with self-pity. I questioned why God would give me another baby now that I was finally going to have some precious time to myself. But in the midst of the endless laundry a new question entered my thoughts. What gift could I develop that would be more important than the gift that God was forming within me? For me, that was a life-changing question. I clearly remember making a choice to trust God to develop all of His *gifts* within me.

When our son was born we named him Jon, which means "God's gracious gift." When he started kindergarten I realized how empty that time would have been without Jon's laughter and tears. In due time I did go back to school to develop some of my other gifts.

God knows my innermost being. He knows better than I what will fill me with joy and bring me eternal pleasure. I can only know my past and present. God knows my future. The best choice I made was to trust Him.

*Lord, You are the Creator, the developer of all that is truly lasting. You are the giver of life and of all good gifts. Help me to develop the most important and lasting gifts You have given me. Thank You for the gifts of love and life. Amen.*

Carolyn Henderson is a graphic designer by profession who enjoys painting, quilting, and writing. She and her husband have three children and make their home in Newbury Park, California.

# The Rainbow of His Love

**Daisy Hepburn**

*He will be like rain falling on a mown field, like showers watering the earth.* Psalm 72:6, *NIV*

We spent four years in lovely Puerto Rico. One of the things I learned to tolerate was constant, unexpected, tropical rain showers. At first, I considered it a nuisance. If we were having a backyard Bible club, our crafts were spoiled. If I had just had my hair done, I was instantly transformed to the wet-mop look.

Eventually, however, we learned to behave like the natives. We didn't even bother with umbrellas but went on about our business and pretended it wasn't happening. Soon, I became grateful for refreshing rain and the lush greenery it produced.

One day, our seven-year-old son came running into the house and said, "Mama, Mama, come quick and look!"

I followed him outside and saw something I had

never seen before and have never seen since. In the sky above us was the complete circle of a rainbow! It was as if God had carefully placed a halo of color above His creation. It made me think of the contrast between God's view and our own.

We see our world blackened with sin and its consequences. Often, from our perspective, it doesn't look all that good. But God sees everything through the prism of His love. He mixes rain with sunshine. And the result is the awesome beauty of His design on creation's canvas.

I'm so grateful to live on this side of Calvary. Because of who Jesus is, you and I can say, "Thank you, Lord, that we're part of the blood-washed church." God sees us through the righteousness of Jesus Christ, through the rainbow of His love.

*Dear Lord, thank You for the rainbow of Jesus' love. Amen.*

Daisy Hepburn is a popular conference and retreat speaker. She is the author of *What's So Glorious About Everyday Living?* and *Look, You're a Leader*. She and her husband, David, have two grown children. The Hepburns make their home in San Francisco, California.

The narrative for this devotion was excerpted from *What's So Glorious About Everday Living* by Daisy Hepburn, published by Here's Life Publishers, San Bernardino, CA, © 1991. Used by permission.

# Precious Moments

**Kathleen Hershey**

*Be still and know that I am God.*
Psalm 46:10, *NIV*

I remember with awe the stars of a blue-black summer night when I was a child. I used to think it was just the heat and humidity of the southern summertime that drove Daddy out into the cool darkness. He'd spread a quilt across the grass, tugging here and there to make it lay flat. Then he'd lie down with his hands under his head and look up at the stars. Always eager to be with him, I'd lie down too, hands under my head, looking up. It was hard to find a place in our yard where there weren't sprays of pine needles or dogwood branches overhead obscuring the view. But Daddy had found his special place with a clear view of the sky. He always spread the quilt there.

"Stars are the windows of heaven," he told me. And I remember thinking then how splendid heaven must be beyond those distant windows.

Years later, with children of my own and living in Southern California, I served as a counselor at church camp. I had a cabin of teenage girls, a discussion group to lead, and a myriad of other responsibilities. Time was a precious commodity as I hurried up a dusty path to the cabin on urgent business. Suddenly I thought I heard someone call "Stop!" I stopped. I looked around.

I was alone on the path that rose above the small stream near the berry bushes with the ladybugs. I stood facing the tree-covered mountain. Quite unexpectedly words from the Psalms came into my mind. "Be still and know that I am God." I'd found another special place and a brief time that would be imprinted on my soul.

After many years away, I walked through the red, yellow, orange, and speckled leaves of a woods in North Carolina. Moss grew on the shaded bark. Swords of sunbeams pierced the leafy ceiling. Bird songs rang and creek water splashed musically. No amount of time in a man-made cathedral could match such special moments.

Time. Special moments in my life's time. Too often I hurry through my day without seeing the wonder of God's world. I neglect to budget my time as carefully as I budget my checkbook. I forget to "Be still ..."

Maybe tonight I'll just step outside under the stars and find my special place to spread my quilt for a moment—one precious moment.

*Dear Lord, help me as I race through my busy days to be still and commune with You. Amen.*

Kathleen Hershey has written mysteries as well as children's stories and verse and a children's book. She has served as a lay speaker and enjoys reading and raising several varieties of birds. Kathleen and her husband have five grown children and reside in Valencia, California.

# Follow the Director

**Barbara Hibschman**

*Rest in the Lord and wait patiently
for Him.* Psalm 37:7, *NASB*

Oh, Mom, please pray I won't
mess up," pleaded Christy, our fifth-grade flutist.

"I'm sure you'll do fine. Just remember to follow
the director," I cautioned as we walked toward the
school gym to attend the spring musical.

I found a seat near the front of the auditorium
and sat with the other parents of the novice
musicians. Sounds of discord filled the air as the
fifth- and sixth-grade band members tuned their
instruments.

Soon the director stepped onto the podium and
lifted his baton. Every instrument moved into a
position that showed it was ready to be played. All
eyes were on the director as they anticipated the
motion of his baton. At the first downbeat the
children attacked the beginning note in unison. As
they continued to follow his leading, a beautiful,
familiar love song emerged.

About halfway through the song, I noticed the director trying to get the attention of a trumpet player who must have been distracted. He had continued to play when he should have rested, so he played a couple of loud measures all by himself. As soon as he realized his mistake, he stopped playing, looked at the director, waited for his cue, and came in at the right place with the other trumpets. The mistake was quickly corrected and the song went on to a peaceful, satisfying ending. The overall performance was wonderful, and we the proud parents applauded profusely.

Sometimes life is like the performance of that song. Failure, gossip, a cutting remark, losses, or rejection by a spouse or children are a few of the distractions that come into view and take our eyes away from our director, the Lord Jesus Christ. But as soon as we realize we're not following His leading, we can stop and look to Him. His strength, love, and grace are sufficient to get us back into the song of living.

*Dear Lord, thank You for covering my mistakes (sins) by Your performance of love on Calvary. Help me to follow You so my day-to-day performance will be a love song to You. Amen.*

Barbara Hibschman has published several articles, short stories, and poems. She is a speaker for women's retreats and writers' conferences and enjoys reading, traveling, playing the piano, and singing. She and her husband, Jim, have two children and live in Warren, New Jersey.

# Wonderfully Made!

**Donna Hislop**

*I praise you because I am fearfully
and wonderfully made; your works
are wonderful, I know that full well.*
Psalm 139:14, *NIV*

Without her even knowing it, my precious daughter Carolyn has been teaching me profound spiritual lessons since her birth just twenty-one months ago.

Although Carolyn weighed only five pounds when I brought her home from the hospital, she quickly became a downright rotund infant. But did she mind that she had a thicker waistline and chunkier cheeks than other babies? Not a bit!

Was she concerned when she took forever to learn to roll over, was late sitting up, and at eighteen months still did not walk on her own? Not at all.

Was she envious of her two-year-old playmate? He sported a $110 snowsuit and a $45 leather aviator jacket last winter. She got by with a coat and snow pants that didn't match and that cost me $7.50

at a used-clothing sale. She didn't even notice.

I am not so presumptuous as to think my toddler is gifted with exceptional spiritual insight. She is simply unconscious of the differences between herself and other children.

Couldn't I learn to be a little more unconscious of the differences between me and other women too?

I could stop checking around the swimming pool to see who looks best in a bathing suit. I could train myself not to be frustrated that I am clumsy with crafts and musical instruments. I don't have to feel intimidated around women who have a flair for fashion and manage to keep their hair smartly styled and their fingernails long and polished.

Yes, I could relax and praise God because I am wonderfully made—even with my tendency toward a pot belly, weak fingernails, and a lack of artistic talent. I give glory to God for the majestic mountains, thundering oceans, fascinating animals, and intricate plants He has created. Am I a less wonderful work than these?

*Father and Creator, help me to rejoice in what You have made of me. Help me to believe that I, too, am one of Your wonderful works. Amen.*

Donna Hislop has written articles for the Christian and secular markets and a handbook on raising money for charity for a national organization. She enjoys reading, baking, and calligraphy. Donna and her husband have two daughters and make their home in Newtown Square, Pennsylvania.

# The Walk

**Janet Hitchman**

*For you have delivered my soul from
death and my feet from stumbling,
that I may walk before God in the
light of life.* Psalm 56:13, *NIV*

I slammed the door behind me,
punctuating my frustration. Why had I asked my
husband to walk with me? After forty-four years of
marriage, I should understand that he does not care
for my spontaneous walks.

Storming up the street, I chose the highest hill in
town. My mind slipped into old patterns of negative
thinking. *It seems like I'm always alone. If only
things were different now that we're retired. How I
wish my husband enjoyed walking with me! I get
tired of doing things by myself.*

Thoughts of self-pity tumbled through my mind.
A car approached me, and a woman called out, "Can
I give you a lift?"

Laughing, I answered, "No thanks. I need the
exercise and time to talk things over with the Lord."
She said she understood and drove off.

Suddenly I was aware of the rain, a cooling patter

on my face. Then I heard the Lord speak to my heart. "Janet, I will never leave you. Have you forgotten the valleys I have led you through, the hills we've climbed together?"

As He spoke, my anger and frustration left. "Oh, Lord, forgive me for expecting my husband to fill all my needs. Thank You for not allowing me to stay trapped in old feelings of self-pity."

Reaching the top of the hill, a great joy filled me as I rested in the Lord's love and forgiveness. He took my hand and we started down the hill towards the new adventure He had for me.

*Thank You, Lord, for all the walks we've taken together, where You have renewed my mind, picked me up, and helped me conquer my fears. Thank You for taking my hand, asking only that I trust in You. Amen.*

Janet Hitchman enjoys gardening, walking, entertaining, teaching Bible studies, and counseling. She is just beginning her article-writing career having previously published her poetry. Janet and her husband, Leonard, have three grown sons and make their home in Kingston, Washington.

# Dinner for Seven

**Darlene Hoffa**

*My cup overflows.* Psalm 23:5, *NIV*

That Saturday afternoon I could barely wait until my young charges' parents showed up to claim them. In a moment of compassion, I had volunteered to keep three preschoolers for two days. While I am not normally prone to offer long-term baby-sitting, this family's plight pulled at my heartstrings.

A traffic accident several months earlier had left the father almost completely paralyzed. Although the brave couple struggled heroically to cope with the tragedy, the burden was overwhelming. And so I decided to give the parents some quiet hours together and the children a break from the sadness at home. Now I was ready to give them back.

Rubbing my aching back, I looked at the clock and thought, *They should be here any minute. Be glad you don't have to prepare dinner.*

Just then, a car drove in. Within minutes, the young couple showed they needed some transition time before taking their brood home. A quick prayer ascended. "We have a challenge, Lord. Please send help fast. What do You suggest I serve this bunch?"

I headed for the freezer. Inside was a pound of hot dogs and a loaf of bread. Scanning the cupboards I discovered a can of chili, two cans of corn, and a package of macaroni and cheese mix. This was getting exciting. Next, I located new jars of peanut butter and jelly. I wasn't sure this covered the four food groups, but it would do. And, wonder of wonders, a full package of Oreo cookies had escaped my cookie-loving family. This would make a perfect dessert. Dinner was complete.

I've served lots of people around our table. I've made detailed lists, shopped carefully, and cooked long hours. But never have I felt the warmth we shared around that simple meal. We laughed, told stories, and shed some tears over the closeness we enjoyed within the circle of Jesus' love.

The crisis was not over for the family, and I, too, would face problems down the road. But that night around our humble kitchen table, we found God's provision more than met our need.

*Dearest Father, thank You for being El Shaddai, the Almighty God, our nourisher and strength giver. Thank You for opening the doors of Your home, through Jesus, inviting us to bring our soul's hunger to You and be satisfied. Amen.*

Darlene Hoffa has had three books published as well as several articles and devotions. She enjoys traveling, walking, reading, and working as lay counselor. Darlene and her husband have three grown children and reside in Brea, California.

# Stand Tall!

## Barbara J. Hyatt

*The Lord is my strength and my
shield, my heart trusteth in him and
I am helped; therefore my heart
greatly rejoiceth and with my song
will I praise him.* Psalm 28:7, *KJV*

Some birthday this is going to be,
I thought, as I looked out the window of the aircraft.

I had always dreamed of celebrating "the big one"
with my much-loved family and dear friends back
home in Washington state, and I was on my way to
do just that. Yet here I was feeling so gloomy. I
continued to peer out the window so no one would
see the tears that began to roll down my cheeks.

Recent misunderstandings with others had
clouded my joy. I felt robbed of the peace that had
once been mine. Here it was, the day before my
birthday; I should have been jumping with joy, at
least feeling some excitement. Instead, I felt sadness
and was crying!

I took paper and pen out of my purse to express
some of what I was feeling. After writing several
pages, I penned: *Dear God, give me some special days*

*with my family and friends. Right now I feel like a wounded soldier crawling on the battlefield of life. Please comfort me in my pain and sorrow.*

Soon after, as I sat in prayer, my answer came: *Barbara, stand up, do not crawl, stand with your head up and march forward!*

As I continued to focus on God, I received renewed strength.

The next day at my birthday celebration, while my loved ones sang "Happy birthday to you!" I wanted to bolt out of my chair and stand tall. But, then, who would have understood?

*Thank You, Lord, that amid life's struggles I can stand up and go forward, experiencing victory instead of defeat. Help me to remember that while disappointments may come from those around me, my strength comes from You. Amen.*

Barbara J. Hyatt is a speaker for Christian Women's Club and a professional floral designer. She and her husband, Stan, have three grown daughters and make their home in Camarillo, California.

# Good-bye, Georgie

**Connie Isakson**

*Bring joy to your servant, for to you,*
*O Lord, I lift up my soul.*
Psalm 86:4, *NIV*

Okay, take Georgie to the Humane Society," I hissed at my husband, after tiring of his coercion.

It wasn't a good time for making decisions. For five months I had been making frequent trips to visit my dying father. Between trips, I had rummaged through ten years of accumulation in preparation for a long-distance move.

Packed and ready to travel a week after my father's death, I was too exhausted to fool with a dog or argue with my husband.

We unloaded our furnishings and settled into our tiny apartment 1,500 miles from home; but once my nest was arranged and fluffed, an intense loneliness tormented me. Not only was I grieving for my father, friends, and familiar surroundings, my faithful little dog no longer shadowed my every move. Nor was she there to curl up beside me and sympathize with my tears.

After a long, miserable week, I phoned my mother-in-law. "Please call the Humane Society and see if we can get Georgie back," I begged.

I fidgeted and fussed, awaiting the return call. "She's been adopted," came the report, "but the woman is willing to return her, although she and Georgie seem to be happy together."

The money involved in retrieving my pet, as well as the trauma it would put her through, caused considerable deliberation. After much prayer, I decided to leave her in her new home and move on with my life as best I could.

A schedule for summer school at the local university arrived a few days later. I enrolled, grateful that my goal for more education could commence so expeditiously. Soon my life was rich and full again, although waves of grief occasionally erupted.

Giving up my special companion of many years proved to be intensely painful, but God was faithful to return joy in the face of my loss. He cares about all the tiny broken places in my heart and fills the cracks with Himself.

*Thank You, Lord, for caring when I hurt. Help me to faithfully lift up my soul to You and receive Your joy. Amen.*

Connie Isakson has written several articles and testimonials of others. She enjoys music, reading, hiking and walking, and has a special interest in missions. Connie and her husband have a grown son and daughter and make their home in Gig Harbor, Washington.

# Out of the Mouths of Babes

**Bonnie Jamison**

*You saw me before I was born and
scheduled each day of my life before I
began to breathe. Every day was
recorded in your Book!*
Psalm 139:16, *TLB*

What grandmother doesn't love to hear of the accomplishments of her grandchild? I was no exception the day my daughter-in-law phoned to say Jenna, age three, had something she wanted to tell me.

"Grammy," she said, "God loved us and sent His Son, First John 4:10, and I'm gonna get a sticker!" Her words, unmistakably clear, thrilled her and overwhelmed me. "Thank You, Lord; surely You are scheduling her days."

The night before our phone coversation, Jenna had attended AWANA Cubbies for the first time. This program is designed to teach little ones the joy of the Lord. Several months later I was invited to attend with her.

When animated Cubbies crowd together in a colorful church room, a miracle seems to happen. Enthralled, they stay through two action-packed hours of learning biblical truths. I marveled at the diligence of the leaders as they lovingly listened to each child's memory verse.

I focused my video camera hoping to get a few good shots of Jenna. Zooming in, I watched seriousness frame her flawless little face as she recited her verse. After the guide praised her work, Jenna looked toward me with dancing eyes, grinning proudly. Again, I was awestruck at seeing the living God use a small child to speak His Word! Clearly His hand was upon her life. There are no words to describe the wonder of a little one already knowing Christ's love.

Thinking back to the day I learned of Jenna's impending birth, memories flooded my mind. Almost at once I had begun to pray that her parents would guide her to Jesus at an early age. Since she was our first grandchild, we searched for the perfect gift; we gave her a white Bible, inscribed with her name, and underlined Psalm 139.

What a privilege to pray for God's guidance upon children's lives even before they are born and then to have the joy of watching His handiwork unfold! Nothing could be more precious.

*Dear Father, in a world where unborn babies are disposed of with impunity, remind me daily of the value of individual lives. Thank You for answered prayer in those You've entrusted to me. May their eyes behold You as they watch my life. Amen.*

Bonnie Jamison is the author of one book and numerous articles and is a frequent speaker for Christian Women's Clubs. Bonnie enjoys reading, walking, biking, interior decorating, and video photography. She and her husband have three grown children and reside in Medford, New Jersey.

# Where Will Daddy Sleep?

**Sandie Jarvis-Dye**

*In my distress I called upon the
LORD ... he heard my voice.*
Psalm 18:6, *KJV*

With no furniture inside our low-income housing apartment, the back porch provided the only seating for me and my three-year-old son Jimmy.

"Let's tie your shoes now; then we'll walk to the hospital and see Daddy again. The doctor said he can come home soon."

"Where will Daddy sleep, Mama?" Jimmy looked at me with wide, green eyes too young and innocent to be so concerned. Still healing from a broken back, Daddy couldn't sleep on the floor like we did.

"I don't know yet, but God does, so we don't need to worry. Remember, we prayed and asked Him for some furniture." I hugged Jimmy reassuringly. He was satisfied and ran toward the sandbox.

"I want to trust You that completely, Lord, but sometimes it's hard," I prayed as I sat on the porch step. "Please forgive me for getting impatient. I know You'll provide for our needs."

"Good morning, isn't this a lovely day?"

I turned and smiled at a little redheaded lady I'd never seen before. After exchanging names, to my amazement, she simply asked me if I could use some furniture.

Hardly believing my ears, I managed to blurt out, "Well ... yes ... I mean, I don't have any!"

"You're an answered prayer," she gently informed me. I didn't understand.

Later, as we sipped tea in her apartment, sitting on the couch that would soon be mine, my new friend shared her story. After finally discovering the perfect house for their family of seven, she and her husband had signed the papers just hours before learning he had lost his job. With no apparent way to make payments on the completely furnished house, her prayer had been simple and direct:

"Lord, if You show me someone who needs my furniture, I'll give it to them and we'll take the house on faith that You'll provide a way to pay for it."

"Daddy, you have a nice bed upstairs to sleep in," explained Jimmy, grabbing my husband's hand and pulling him toward the stairway. Jim had just been released from the hospital, walked into a completely furnished home, and shook his head in wonder at this God in whom his wife placed so much faith.

A redheaded lady across town (whose husband's job had just been reinstated) and a thankful lady at our house didn't wonder at all. Neither did the little blond boy. After all, hadn't we asked?

171

*Thank You, Lord, that I can always call on You for help and know You will hear and that I can confidently teach my children to trust in You. Amen.*

Sandie Jarvis-Dye has written several articles and Sunday School take-home papers. She enjoys music, gardening, and teaching Bible Club. Sandie has four grown children. She and her husband live in East Wenatchee, Washington.

# An Opportunity Revisited

**Gail D. Johnsen**

*Declare his glory among the nations,
his marvelous deeds among all
peoples.* Psalm 96:3, *NIV*

I browsed through the shoe
department looking at the selection of running shoes.
Did the puzzled look on my face prompt the young
salesgirl to ask if she could help?

"Yes, please. I am looking for a pair of running
shoes for my husband."

She showed me a few styles and then suggested it
might be better if he could come in and try them on
himself.

"Well, they're a surprise for our anniversary," I
explained.

"Oh," she perked up. "How long have you been
married?"

"Eleven years."

"Eleven years! That's almost a record nowadays! How did you do it?"

"Well ... ah ... ," I stammered. "A lot of hard work, I guess."

She smiled, nodded, and finished my purchase transaction. I thanked her, stuffed the gift under my arm, and walked away.

I strolled the mall corridor feeling unsettled with our conversation. I wished I'd said things differently. What I really wanted to say was that Jesus Christ is the One who has made all the difference in our lives. Because of Him our marriage has not only survived but has flourished. I'd had an opportunity to proclaim the name of Jesus but lost it.

I walked into another store and fumbled halfheartedly through the blouses, then darted out and started back to the shoe department.

The young woman was still there. Alone.

"Excuse me," I said. "Remember me? I was just here."

"Oh, yes," she smiled, "The running shoes and the anniversary."

"I have something to tell you," I started. "What I told you earlier about my marriage was a lie."

Her eyes widened.

"I mean, I didn't tell you the whole truth. Eleven years of marriage does take a lot of hard work. But what has kept us together during the hard times has been our commitment to Jesus Christ. Because of our relationship with Jesus we can have a lasting and fulfilling relationship with each other."

Tears came to her eyes and she thanked me for sharing. She said she and her husband were going through some difficulties. She thanked me again and turned away.

We never know the impact we can have when we

make Jesus known to others. Let's not be ashamed, but boldly share His love with those we come in contact with. We possess the words of life in a lost and dying generation.

*Lord, give me a love for people, a passion for lost souls, and a boldness to share Your love with those I meet each day. Amen.*

Gail D. Johnsen is a published writer who enjoys reading, sewing, running, and cross-country skiing. In addition, Gail is a teacher/speaker for her adult Sunday School and ladies' ministries group and a home schooler. She and her husband have two children and reside in Auburn, Washington.

# *Life is Hard, and Then ...*

**Barbara Johnson**

*Precious in the sight of the Lord is*
*the death of His godly ones.*
Psalm 116:15, *NASB*

For two hours I had been doing the talk show, and I had told my radio host and all the people who had called in just about everything I knew. We were almost out of time when the host turned to me and said, "Barbara, we have just two minutes left—if you could say one thing to encourage all the people who are listening, what would you say?"

I felt a twinge of panic. I wasn't sure I could even think of my name, and I had already said everything I knew—I couldn't even think of a Scripture verse. I glanced into the little Joy Box I take with me when I'm interviewed to see if there was anything left among my props that might give our radio audience some encouragement. Then I gleefully found one bumper snicker that I hadn't used, and I said, "Well, there is one thing I would like to tell everyone, and it's this: 'LIFE IS HARD, AND THEN YOU DIE.'"

The shocked host of the show looked at me as if I had lost every marble I had.

"Well ... UH ... Barbara ... maybe you could tell us in a few seconds why you think that's encouraging ..." he stammered.

I could tell my host was thinking, "What is she going to do NOW?" I wasn't sure either, but I plunged in.

"What I mean is, our EXIT from this life is our GRANDEST ENTRANCE up there. This life isn't it! There is pain and suffering ... but those who want to name it and claim it are looking in the wrong place because there is nothing here to name and claim! This isn't it!

"This life is hard. There are all kinds of pain, there are all kinds of problems—AIDS, divorce, crime, disease ... sin. Life is hard, and some of the people listening know how hard it can be. But I like what my little granddaughter told me: 'Grandma, you shouldn't say life is hard and then you die; you should say life is hard and then you GET TO DIE.'

"I really believe that's good news for Christians. We have an ENDLESS HOPE, not a HOPELESS END and, while life is hard, someday we will die, which isn't really bad—it simply means we'll leave this life and go to be with our Lord and Savior, and what could be better than that?

"That's why I believe in rapture practice ... I go out in the backyard and jump up and down, practicing for the rapture, because one day we'll soon be out of here. I love that song, 'I'll Fly Away,' because I know my future is so secure with Him. This life holds no charm for me ... my deposits are in heaven, just waiting for me to come! What a day it will be when we cast our crowns at His feet. This life is just a veil of tears, but earth has no sorrow that heaven cannot heal. Life is hard and tough, but it is only temporary ... this life is only a vapor, but eternity is FOREVER!"

*Heavenly Father, thank You for the reminder that the pain and suffering we experience today are only temporary and that one day we who call upon the name of Your Son will have the privilege of entering into the gates of Your eternal presence. Amen.*

Barbara Johnson is a humorist and much sought-after conference speaker. She is the founder of Spatula Ministries and the author of *Where Does a Mother Go to Resign?, Fresh Elastic for Stretched Out Moms,* and her latest best-seller *So, Stick a Geranium in Your Hat and Be Happy!*

The narrative for this devotion was excerpted from the book *So, Stick a Geranium in Your Hat and Be Happy!* by Barbara Johnson, published by Word, Inc., Irving, TX, © 1990. Used by permission.

# Midweek Miseries

## Carolyn Johnson

*Find rest, O my soul, in God alone;*
*my hope comes from him.*
Psalm 62:5, *NIV*

**D**epression stalks me. Gloom
hovers around the fringes of my days. It creeps up
behind me like a thief and overtakes me at last on a
morning like this. My alarm rings and I don't want
to get out of bed. I look out at the fog and feel too
tired to go for my morning walk. I remember a lunch
date with a friend and think about canceling and
staying home.

*Lord, what's wrong with me? You have blessed me*
*with so much--a loving family, good friends, material*
*things. I thought my blue moods would disappear*
*forever when I became a Christian. What happened to*
*the joy of my salvation? Where is the inspiration I felt*
*at church on Sunday? Lord, are You there? I need to*
*feel Your presence on this dreary Wednesday.*

I get up, walk, have lunch with my friend. We
talk to each other about moods. My friend says
maybe ...

It's the weather; they've done scientific studies;

179

It's your age; the menopause, you know;

It's something you're suppressing from your childhood.

I go home and find a new women's magazine in the mailbox. I take it and curl up in the old lounge chair. Maybe there's a helpful article, an absorbing story, a new recipe. The table of contents is disappointing. I flip through the pages, looking at the slender models in their beautiful clothes and the elegant rooms in the home decorating section.

I put the magazine aside and wander into the front hall. There amid the clutter is my Bible, where I left it on Sunday after church. I open it to the place I'd marked during the sermon and begin to read from the book of Hebrews:

> And since we have a great priest over the house of God, let us draw near to God with a sincere heart in full assurance of faith.... Let us hold unswervingly to the hope we profess, for he who promised is faithful (10:21-23).

I draw near.

*Lord, forgive me for not opening Your Word sooner. Your love is greater than dreary weather or hormonal changes or hidden memories. Thank You for coming close again. Amen.*

Carolyn Johnson has had articles published in various magazines and is the author of two books. She enjoys motor-home traveling, visiting family and friends, and church and community activities. The Johnsons have a blended family of nine grown children and reside in Solvang, California.

# Assuming
# the Best

**Jan Johnson**

*Blessed is he who has regard for the
weak; the Lord delivers him in times
of trouble.* Psalm 41:1, *NIV*

As the remaining seats filled and
overflowed, I felt uncomfortable sitting on one of the
soft green sofas.

"All of you younger gals, please sit on the floor,"
the women's retreat leader chirped. I was a younger
gal, but I didn't move.

Since we had just joined this church, none of
these ladies knew about the multiple leg fractures I'd
received in an auto accident a year before. I've
always camouflaged my stiff knee and hid the long
purple scars on my ankle.

Now, I was afraid that no one would understand
why I didn't offer my seat to someone else. Would
these women think the church's newest member was
selfish?

I thought about sitting on the floor anyway. I
looked for a place to sit with a stable object I could

use to raise myself up on. I didn't see one. Besides, it would create a dramatic little scene as I tried to maneuver my stiff right leg into position. I knew better than to force wobbly joints to do tricks in front of people. I sat tight.

It would have been easier if I were still using crutches. Then people would understand why I nested my right foot on an extra chair in front of me during the teaching sessions. Now, without my wooden props, I looked whole again even though I wasn't.

I opened my Bible and hid there until everyone was settled. There, I talked with God silently, confident that He understood.

How many people have I considered selfish because of some outward activity? I asked Him. What unseen injuries were plaguing that grumpy older person, that new mother, that worn out minister--all of whom I'd criticized? Were they weak in spirit while I was weak in body? Were they recuperating from some devastating personal injury?

I vowed anew to give people the benefit of the doubt. I resolved to curb my overworked analytical powers and assume the best about others.

*Help me to give other people the benefit of the doubt, Lord. Don't let me shoot a wounded person even if their wounds are invisible to me. Amen.*

Jan Johnson is the author of numerous magazine articles, adult Bible study curriculum, and two books, *When It Hurts to Grow* and *Creating a Safe Place: Christians Healing from the Hurt of Dysfunctional Families.* Jan and her husband, Greg, have two children and reside in Simi Valley, California.

# *Just Say No!*

## Carole Turner Johnston

*I will set before my eyes no vile thing.*
Psalm 101:3, *NIV*

I heard one bad word and decided to wait and see if there were others. My eight-year-old daughter had planned on this movie for over a week, and so had I. Watching it would also give me a little reprieve from mothering on this humid August evening. Oh, how I hoped I would hear no more foul language!

But even as I waited, the war was on. My own sense of right and wrong had already been violated. I didn't really want proof, I wanted an excuse—and my well-earned quiet time.

While I was in such a quandary, one of those anti-drug commercials about brains frying away on drugs came on. And I wondered for the hundredth time why anyone would continue or even start on drugs when it was so obviously wrong.

Wrong? Obvious? Why, I was in the same position here. I had other choices, wholesome ones, yet I was playing with the truth, trying to stretch it for my own benefit, forgetting the commitment I had made earlier in the week.

It was the Monday reading from Psalm 101, and I had even made a note in my journal: *I will set before my eyes no vile thing.* And I had signed it.

Slowly I repeated the verse to myself and, knowing that I would have to stem my daughter's disappointment as well as my own and explain my backing down on a promise, firmly switched off the TV.

I was surprised.

"It had bad language in it, didn't it, Mother?" Her response was simple and direct. "I think I'll play outside before it gets dark." And off she went.

I hadn't had to deliver a sermon on the subject; Jennifer had her own sense of right and wrong. Maybe my new resolution wouldn't be so hard to keep after all.

*Dear Lord, help me to remember that my daily choices will be much easier if I refer back to Your Word and count on You for wisdom. Please give me the courage to say no to unhealthy choices and yes to those that honor You. Amen.*

Carole Turner Johnston has written greeting cards, poetry, articles, and devotions. Besides writing, she enjoys teaching Sunday School, taking walks, and exploring nature. Carole and her husband, Terry, have three sons and two daughters. The Johnstons reside in Onawa, Iowa.

# A New Song

**Debbie Kalmbach**

*He put a new song in my mouth, a*
*hymn of praise to our God.*
Psalm 40:3, *NIV*

Pain. The raw, aching stiffness. I can't remember what it was like not hurting; to move freely, not calculating each step. Doctors say I must learn to live with it. Medical technology doesn't have the answers. The damage is done.

Forever. A cruel, unjust sentence. How could a simple fall on an icy sidewalk cause a permanent injury? I want to scream, "It isn't fair!"

I miss brisk early morning walks, the wind in my face when I jogged, hikes on mountain trails. I grieve for the way it was before the accident.

I struggle with awkward feelings. I'm still self-conscious of my slow, uneven gait. Many nights I've gone to bed weary from the pain, wondering how I'll face another day, much less a whole lifetime. "Lord, I don't think I can do it. It's too hard."

As I become still, God's gentle voice speaks to my heart. "I will teach you new songs, songs of joy, not sadness. I will be your strength. My grace is all you need."

Time brings acceptance, but it's a slow process. I press forward, slip back, then forge ahead as I gain insight into God's ways. I sing different songs. Days aren't as hurried now. Priorities are more focused. I allow time to curl up with a book, to rest and be renewed. I'm learning to manage the pain. Forever is only today, and God has promised sufficient grace. With His strength I'll make it, one day at a time.

*Dear Lord, I confess I don't understand Your ways. I rail against the pain, the disappointments, the limitations. Yet You are faithful. Though my life has changed, You're teaching me the words to new songs, songs of praise for lessons learned. I choose to sing them, finding contentment and joy for each new day. Amen.*

Debbie Kalmbach is a published writer who enjoys quiet moments for reading and writing, drives on country roads, and music. She and her husband, Randy, have two sons and make their home in Auburn, Washington.

# Hungry, Anyone?

**Nancy Kennedy**

*You still the hunger of those you
cherish.* Psalm 17:14, *NIV*

Yesterday I woke up hungry. I
wandered into the kitchen and poured myself a big
bowl of cereal. I popped two pieces of bread into the
toaster and turned on the coffee maker. A glass of
orange juice and a half of a banana completed my
breakfast. I ate every bit of it, yet remained
unsatisfied and restless. I grabbed a handful of
pretzels and sat down with a stack of magazines and
another cup of coffee.

I must have leafed through a dozen magazines,
but nothing interested me. Besides, I had a gnawing
hunger inside. I poured another cup of coffee and
called my friend Joanne.

Normally, Joanne and I could chat for hours, but
yesterday I couldn't concentrate. I still felt hungry,
despite everything I'd nibbled on all morning.

"You've got to keep your hands busy or you'll eat
everything in sight," I scolded myself. I picked up my

cross-stitching project and sat down to sew. After only a dozen or so stitches, I set it down and turned on the TV.

"Ah, a cooking show!" My mouth watered as my bearded TV friend prepared chicken potpies.

"Pie! That will surely hit the spot." I grabbed my purse and drove to the mall. Once there, I sat at the counter of the pie shop and savored every last forkful of a slice of berry pie. When I got up to leave, I felt full but not quite satisfied. So I strolled for awhile throughout the mall.

An hour later, I tossed a shopping bag containing a pair of jeans I didn't need and a T-shirt I didn't really like into the backseat of my car and drove home to fix dinner.

No sooner had I finished the dinner dishes than I was up roaming the house, restless—and still hungry. I nibbled on a bowlful of popcorn all evening until I fell into bed at ten o'clock.

I stared at the ceiling, wide awake—still hungry. I tiptoed into the kitchen and stared into my open refrigerator.

It wasn't food I hungered for. Neither was it new clothes, entertainment, busy work for my hands, nor even sleep.

"Oh, Lord," I prayed. "I'm hungry for You. Will You feed me?"

I opened His Word and had myself a feast. He met me at my kitchen table—me, whom He cherishes. He stilled my hungering heart with Himself.

I went back to bed, satisfied.

*Lord, every time I find myself trying to fill my hunger with earthly things, point me back to You, for You alone bring satisfaction. Amen.*

Nancy Kennedy is the author of several articles and poems and a book of humorous writings to be published by Evergreen in 1992. Nancy enjoys making country stuffed animals, dried flower wreaths, and collecting grapevine baskets. She and her husband, Barry, have two daughters and make their home in Inverness, Florida.

# *In the Day of Trouble*

**Agnes Cunningham Lawless**

*Call upon me in the day of trouble; I
will deliver you, and you will honor
me.* Psalm 50:15, *NIV*

It was a chilly, gray morning in
Brunswick, Maine, where my retired husband, John,
and I cared for his ailing, elderly mother. I carried
breakfast to her room and set it on a TV tray before
her. A tiny lady, my mother-in-law sat in an
overstuffed chair, propped up with pillows.

She picked up the spoon and slowly stirred her
oatmeal, then took a bite. "This is cold!" she said
peevishly.

"It was hot when I dished it."

"Take it away! I'm not hungry." She wiped her
mouth and glared at me. "Can't you do anything
right?"

I hurried out and ran upstairs. Throwing myself
on our bed, I cried tears of resentment and self-pity.
John came in and asked, "What happened?"

Between sobs, I told him. "She says such cutting
things! How long do I have to take this?"

"Honey, remember, the ministrokes have affected
her brain. She's just not herself."

I wiped my eyes and joined John in Bible reading.
One verse stood out: "Call upon me in the day of

190

trouble; I will deliver you, and you will honor me."
As we knelt by the bed, I prayed, "Lord, we call upon You in this time of trouble. Help us!" I paused. "And forgive me for getting hurt."

As time passed, Mother gradually grew helpless. She lost her ability to walk, to lift a spoon to her mouth, to talk. The doctor gave her an alphabet card so she could spell out her wishes.

Since she could no longer have her own devotions, we read the Bible and prayed with her every morning. God's love and compassion within me grew. I thought how difficult this illness must be for her.

One afternoon, I sat beside her and fed her like a baby. When I finished, I put my arm around her and said, "I love you."

Reaching for her alphabet card, she spelled out, "I love you too." She looked at me with a radiant smile, her blue eyes flooding with tears.

As I sat holding one of her frail hands, I thought of the verse that had meant so much to me months before: "Call upon me in the day of trouble; I will deliver you." Yes, that was it. I had called on God for help, and He had wonderfully answered.

*Father, help me to call on You whenever I'm in trouble. I know You will hear and answer—in Your time and in Your way. Amen.*

Agnes Cunningham Lawless has coauthored three Bible-study books and written several magazine articles. A board member of the Northwest Christian Writers' Association, she also hosts a writers' group in her home. Agnes enjoys counted cross-stitch and needlepoint embroidery. The Lawlesses have one grown son and live in Bellevue, Washington.

# Faithful—Or Fearful?

**Vivian M. Loken**

*The Lord is my light and my
salvation—whom shall I fear? The
Lord is the stronghold of my life—of
whom shall I be afraid?*
Psalm 27:1, *NIV*

I was at my wits' end. Colleen, a
relative who was feuding with family members,
chose me as her sounding board. I listened to hours
of details about the quarrel, each new development
setting off another descriptive retelling.

"What in the world can I do?" I asked my friend
Bonnie after one long gruelling session.

"Just listen, I guess," she replied sympathetically.
"People who are hurting need to talk to someone and
she's picked you. But you certainly have the right to
tell her when you've had enough."

Feeling somewhat relieved by Bonnie's advice, I
prayed, asking God to show me how I could help, yet
protect myself.

Before long Colleen was back, freshly indignant

over a new report of slander. Her monologue droned on until I excused myself to go start a load of laundry.

Above my laundry tubs is a single light bulb with a chain. As I pulled the chain, light flooded my work area. "If only receiving light on my problems with Colleen were as simple as pulling this chain," I said under my breath.

Almost immediately, I was reminded of a familiar passage of Scripture, "The Lord is my light." There was more, and I probed to remember. "Whom shall I fear?"

As I measured detergent into the washer, I pondered the verse. Fear of what? Was I afraid? Yes, I had to admit that I was. Afraid that not continuing to listen to Colleen would make her angry with me. Afraid, also, that having reached a saturation point, I might lash out and hurt her even more.

Slowly, I walked back upstairs. Although I felt uneasy about telling Colleen my feelings, I was encouraged by the scriptural message that had spoken to me.

As Colleen reopened the case, I said, carefully and gently, "Colleen, I've heard all I can stand for now. Let's make a pact. You can confide in me providing you don't rehash anything. To relive the pain isn't good for you and it puts pressure on me."

Looking forlorn and rejected, Colleen turned to go. With the memory of the light above my laundry tubs fresh in mind, I said, "There's a Bible verse that says, 'The Lord is my light—whom shall I fear?' Maybe that will help you through this feud, Colleen."

Before she left, she smiled meekly and said, "I know you care or you wouldn't try to help me."

*Lord, help me to remember that You are the*

*stronghold of my life and because of that I have*
*nothing to fear. You shed light on all my problems if I*
*but pull the chain and make the connection. Amen.*

Vivian M. Loken has written numerous poems and articles
and has been published in a variety of publications across
the country. She enjoys photography and crocheting afghans.
Vivian and her husband, Donald, have one grown son and
make their home in Minneapolis, Minnesota.

# Trusting in Deep Water

**Yvonne Martinez**

*Since you are my rock and my
fortress, for the sake of your name
lead and guide me.* Psalm 31:3, *NIV*

**M**y sons, ages five and six, were
playing in the pool, splashing, laughing, and having
a great time. Although they had learned to swim the
previous summer, I noticed that they didn't venture
into water over their heads.

I wanted to challenge them with the skills they
had learned, so jumping into the water I gathered
them up and we headed for deeper water. Reaching
the middle of the pool, I encouraged them to let go
and swim to the edge, which was only a few feet
away. Their laughing quickly turned to pleading. As
their grip tightened around my shoulders and neck
they cried, "No, Mommy, please take us back where
we can stand up." Fear, rather than trust, echoed in
their voices.

Didn't they know that I wouldn't let them sink?
My feelings were hurt as I wondered why they didn't
trust me. My reassuring and coaxing had made no
difference at all; finally I ushered them back to the
shallow end.

It was amazing how quickly the playing and laughing resumed. They were secure where they could touch the bottom of the pool. Suddenly I became aware of how like them I was. I, too, liked being comfortable and in control.

I remembered being asked recently to counsel someone with a difficult problem, which I declined because of my lack of confidence. God was asking me to come and swim in deeper waters with Him, but, because I was afraid, I didn't try. What other challenges or opportunities for spiritual growth had I turned down because of fear? Did God's heart also ache when I didn't trust Him? I wanted more than anything for God to lead me, and yet when He tried I chose to stay where I was secure.

Looking into the water, I couldn't help but smile as I thanked God for His love that was so gently correcting me. I asked once again for Him to lead me where He desired. I also asked for the strength to willingly follow.

Just then one of the children jumped up and yelled, "I love you, Mom!" My heart raced with compassion as I chuckled out loud. "I love you too," I shouted back and swam over to them in the shallow water.

*My heart cries to be close and intimate with You, O Lord. Forgive me for not always trusting and following Your perfect leading. Amen.*

Yvonne Martinez is a published writer and speaks nationally for church and ministry groups and retreats. A licensed minister serving as pastoral counselor, she has facilitated support groups for victims for five years. Yvonne and her husband have four children and make their home in Torrance, California.

# *Layer It On*

**Brenda Maxfield**

*Teach me your way, O Lord, and I
will walk in your truth; give me an
undivided heart, that I may fear your
name.* Psalm 86:11, *NIV*

I slung the dishes onto the table
and hollered, "Hurry up! Breakfast is ready. We
haven't much time!"

Nathan came wandering into the kitchen
barefooted, his bleary little eyes still puffy with
sleep.

"Nathan Paul, I told you to get your shoes. Can't
you see Mommy is in a hurry?" I peered down the
hallway. "Bethany! Can't you hear? I said breakfast
is ready."

Nathan stood still, his bare toes planted on the
kitchen linoleum. "Nathan!" I said again. "Your
shoes!" He turned slowly toward his bedroom.

"Just forget it." My voice was like ice. "I'll get
them."

I rushed into his room and dug under the bed,
retrieving his shoes. I also grabbed a pair of socks
and headed back to the kitchen.

"Sit down," I ordered. He did. I crammed each foot quickly into a sock and a shoe.

Bethany still hadn't made her appearance. "BETHANY! WHAT ARE YOU DOING?"

"Coming …" her voice floated back.

"Why are we in a hurry?" Nathan asked.

"Because I have a million and one things to do, not the least of which is to be at a meeting in exactly fifteen minutes." I dashed around the kitchen, dishing up the hot cereal. "It sure would be nice to have some cooperation around here."

Bethany ambled into the kitchen and plopped onto her chair. I scooped another spoon of cereal into her bowl. "What in the world are you wearing?" My eyes crisscrossed over her plaid and flowered outfit.

"Well, they both have blue in them!" she answered indignantly.

"You'll have to change. That looks ridiculous." I glanced at my watch. "Look at the time. Choke it down, kids. Hurry up!"

I threw the pan into the sink and ran to get my Bible and notebook. As I bent to touch my Bible, my hand froze.

Sudden thoughts flooded my mind nearly knocking me over. What was I doing? How was I acting? Jesus never ran around frazzled and nervous, trying to squish too much into life. And look at His mission!

I sank onto the floor. This meeting I had to attend, was it what God wanted me to do? Had I even asked Him? I mean really asked Him and then listened for His answer?

Or had I just presumed and then layered it onto an already full life? I took a deep breath and bowed my head.

There were going to be some changes.

*Dear Father, thank You for Your wisdom. Show me what You want me to do this day. Don't let my heart be divided against Your purposes for me. I pause now to listen. Thank You for speaking. Amen.*

Brenda Maxfield has published several articles and is active in teaching, singing, and playing the piano. She also enjoys reading, taking walks, and going on dates with her husband. She and her husband, Paul, have two children and make their home in Grand Cayman, British West Indies, where they are working in missions.

# Oasis of Peace

**Leslie McLeod**

*My soul thirsts for God, for the living God. When can I go and meet with God?* Psalm 42:2, *NIV*

The dog was wailing in an embarrassing crescendo for dinner. So was the baby. And I could almost hear my husband's stomach growling in chorus. I'd discovered a new wrinkle by my right eye, spent far more than I had intended at the grocery store, and hit the curb in my rush backing into the driveway. It was not a good day.

My parched, war-weary soul gasped for a drink of the Lord's living water; yet, somehow, another day had passed without those peaceful moments of refreshment alone with Him that I so desperately needed.

"Lord," my thoughts burst out that night, "I'm miserable without You. I keep promising to meet with You consistently, but I always fail. Please, help me."

A sweet strain of hope sang to me gently. Christ

is my source, the author of my salvation and of any good work I could ever do. He desires our moments together as fervently as I do; I will look to Him to provide them.

I prayed, "My faithful Lord, You know the needs and desires of my heart. You know my responsibilities and my weaknesses. I am trusting You to set aside a few minutes each day for our time together. I will look for it, and when the first opportunity comes along, I'll use that time You have given for our fellowship."

The quiet refreshment He gives me is like hidden treasure. I may find it first thing in the morning or not until those last moments before bedtime. It may even be just short "sips" throughout the day. I may have to ignore some loud nonessentials, such as laundry, the telephone, the evening news. But every day an oasis of peace is available to me. I have only to seek it!

*Lord, how I thirst for You. Thank You for the gift of Your wonderful, replenishing presence. Amen.*

Leslie McLeod has had several health-related articles published. Besides writing she's "learning the wonderful art of full-time homemaking." She and her husband, Dan, have one daughter and reside in Westminster, California.

# An Appointed Time for Everything

**Cheri Metteer**

*So teach us to number our days, that
we may present to Thee a heart of
wisdom.* Psalm 90:12, *NASB*

The three months following Dad's
death had not been easy for Mother. Seventy-five
years old and no longer the strong person I'd always
known her to be, she was in a confused state of
mind. Daily I stopped to visit her in the retirement
home where she lived.

Twice a week I would help Mother take a shower
bath, which was difficult for me, since this was
something she would never do without my insisting
upon it. Those days were never very pleasant, but no
one else was available to help Mother.

One afternoon I stopped by, knowing it was time
for a shower and dreading it. But this day the Lord
spoke to my heart, "Don't bother with a shower
today; just sit and visit." That day Mother and I had
a great time together as she recalled incidents from

my childhood. We sat and laughed like we hadn't done in years.

I was surprised to hear Mother's voice on the phone at seven the next morning; she usually slept until ten.

"Cheri! I haven't been able to sleep most of the night. I've had this terrible pain in my chest and all down my left arm!"

I recognized the symptoms she described as a heart attack and sent for an ambulance. Mother was rushed to the hospital.

The next two days I was at Mother's side as much as I could be. She slept most of the time and barely recognized me when she was awake. I felt drained as I left the hospital on the second evening to go home and get some rest.

That night I was awakened out of a sound sleep by the phone ringing. "This is the hospital calling; your mother has died."

I knew she was now with the Lord, but grief set in, and I began to cry. Yet how thankful I was for that wonderful last visit we had had on this earth—and for the Lord's prompting to forgo the shower.

*Lord, thank You for Your gentle promptings. Because You know the beginning from the end, I can trust in Your wisdom always. Amen.*

Cheri Metteer, who has written other devotions, enjoys journaling, reading, and attending creative writing classes and writers' conferences. She and her husband, Chuck, have five grown children and make their home in Kirkland, Washington.

# *From Jitters to Joy*

**Lucille Moses**

*If I ride the morning winds to the
farthest oceans, even there your hand
will guide me, your strength will
support me.* Psalm 139:9, *TLB*

Hey, Mom! Guess what?" my
daughter Thelma shouted as she rushed into the
house after school.

"What?" I called from the bedroom.

"Mr. Wallace is going to take our class to
Washington, D.C." She bounced into the room and
plopped herself on the bed. "He wants to do this
every year. Our eighth grade class will be the first
one to go. Neato, huh?"

Her obvious delight was contagious, especially
when she added, "Oh, yeah, Mom, they want you to
be a chaperon."

I felt exhilarated about the opportunity and
happy that Thelma wanted me to accompany her
class. However, after thinking about it, foreboding
began to creep in. The newspapers had recently

reported several crashes. My imagination began flashing pictures of our plane falling enroute, with everyone being killed. I had flown safely several times before. Why did this unreasonable fear now wrap chains around my heart and grip my mind? How could I overcome this consuming terror?

Time closed in. I searched the Scriptures frantically, imploring God to direct me to a verse that would calm my unsettled mind.

Then, one morning I opened *The Living Bible*. The first few verses of Psalm 139 caught my attention. When I came to the ninth verse, the words leaped out at me. "If I ride the morning winds to the farthest oceans, even there your hand will guide me, your strength will support me."

The verse struck home! Thelma's class was scheduled to leave on an early morning flight and cross our country, almost touching another ocean. I read and reread the words. God personally answered me.

Laughing and crying at the release flooding over me, I dropped to my knees, joyfully thanking my heavenly Father. Then I began to prepare for a wonderful trip to our nation's capital, knowing that "even there" I would never be without God's guidance and support.

*Father, thank You for knowing when I feel fear and distress. Thank You for always supplying the answers that will calm my mind and emotions, giving me Your peace and joy. Amen.*

Lucille Moses besides writing enjoys reading, gardening, sewing, and crafts. In addition, she is the registrar for Biola Writers' Institute. Lucille has one grown daughter and makes her home in Fullerton, California.

# Take Time for God

**Joyce Anne Munn**

*My eyes stay open through the
watches of the night, that I may
meditate on your promises.*
Psalm 119:148, *NIV*

**M**y favorite coffee mugs say "I
think I'm allergic to morning" and "I'd enjoy the day
more if it started later." The simple fact is that I'm a
night person. No matter how many hours of sleep I
have, the first few hours after waking I resemble the
hound dog on my cup whose eyes are barely open.

A couple of years ago, an article written by a
Christian doctor upset me greatly. It implied there
was something less spiritual about a person not
willing to get up a little bit earlier than usual in the
morning to spend special time with the Lord.

Was there something wrong with me? I wondered.
Was I slighting my precious Lord with my
selfishness? A short time in the Word and in prayer
convinced me my life was on the right track. There
was no need for me to change my late-hour talks

with the Lord to early morning mutterings. Reading and studying Scripture late at night gave me the opportunity I needed to reflect on the day and relax before getting the rest I needed.

My most important discovery during this time of self-evaluation was the need for more time with the Lord, *whenever* that might be.

How about you? Are you a morning person? Wonderful! Get up and enjoy the beauty of God's creation as it awakens with you. Relax in His love and prepare your heart for the day ahead. Are you a night person? That's great too! Perhaps a special time in the evening with the Lord is the best way to unwind and learn more of His will. Maybe you're thinking it makes no difference if you're a morning or night person. So true! The important thing is to find time somewhere in your hectic schedule to spend alone with God.

Quality time with God must be a priority for continued growth and spiritual strength. But no one can set our times for us; we need to set our own times with God.

*Dear Father, thank You for creating me uniquely. Help me to know the best times to spend quietly with You. And thank You for being ready to hear me anytime, day or night. Amen.*

Joyce Anne Munn is a published writer and enjoys reading, quilling, playing the piano, and working counted cross-stitch. A public school teacher for several years, Joyce also taught for two years in a mission school in Puerto Rico. She makes her home in Watts, Oklahoma.

# Love Undeserved

**Fern Noah**

*For You did form my inward parts,*
*You did knit me together in my*
*mother's womb.* Psalm 139:13, *AMP*

**W**hen our precious daughter
Susan was born, and we were told she had Down
syndrome, my world started to skid down, down,
down to depression and despair. It took some time to
get to know Susan and to appreciate the value and
love that she was bringing into our family.

The hardest to bear was the lack of
understanding by the community. Children stared
with open curiosity. Adults didn't bother to mask
their disapproval at seeing someone so different from
themselves—or their own children. One woman
wondered aloud what awful sin we had committed to
deserve such a child. It took all of the Christian
compassion I could muster to forgive her, realizing
that she had spoken out of ignorance.

Then one day I felt impressed by the Lord to read
Psalm 139 and to consider it as if Susan, herself,

were reading it. Verse 13 in particular caught my attention, and I underlined it.

It said to me that God knew Susan before she was born. He, God our Creator, formed Susan and knit her together in the womb. Therefore, she and others like her have as much reason for existing as the most intelligent among us. Susan has a circle of influence no less important. She has brought love, for she is loving; she has taught trust, for she is trusting.

A dear lady noticed Susan in our car one day as my husband and I were about to leave the shopping center, and she stopped to chat. "She is a pretty girl," she said, nodding toward our daughter. "I have a couple of friends like her, and they are precious."

"Yes," I agreed, grateful that this stranger appreciated Susan. "They have a lot of love to offer."

"Even when we don't deserve it," my husband interjected.

"Yes, indeed," the woman said thoughtfully. "That's a good lesson for all of us."

Susan has taught our family many lessons through the years, but this is the most important: to give love back, even to the undeserving, is a God-like quality. And that very quality could be the best reason for Susan's existence.

*Dear Father in heaven, You have formed each of us for Your own. May we remember that even those who are different have a reason for being and a place in Your kingdom. Amen.*

Fern Noah has written children's stories and devotionals. Her favorite hobbies are sewing, reading, and writing. Fern and her husband, Fred, have three grown children and reside in Grants Pass, Oregon.

# Thank You Anyway, Father

**Patricia Erwin Nordman**

*You will not fear the terror of night.*
Psalm 91:5, *NIV*

His scream on that black December night severed my heart into bleeding halves that wept red agony. The bloodcurdling scream and the gunshot dissolved into death, a finality that seemed impossible, unbelievable.

Chuck was my oldest son. He was nineteen, handsome and brilliant, and in his third year of college, he was full of promise. Psalm 55:4 says, "My heart is in anguish within me." Chuck told me about his anguish three weeks before he did something about it.

Fortunately I already knew a loving God, a Father who watched His own precious Son die. Oh, how that seeped into my crushed heart right after my son's death. It was only then that I finally and fully understood our heavenly Father's total love for us all.

When I was very young, a blessed teacher told me that "Disappointment is His appointment." God's appointment for me was that night. I knew that God's grace is sufficient; that, if I only believed, He could bring me through even the darkest night of my soul.

Grief teaches so many valuable lessons. My first exercise was learning to say, "Thank You, Father." How difficult that was to do, especially amid such searing sorrow! But God's Word says, "Sacrifice thank offerings to God ... and call upon me in the day of trouble; I will deliver you, and you will honor me" (Psalm 50:14-15). To give thanks in such circumstances is indeed a sacrifice, for it would be so easy to ask, "What have I to be thankful for in such a terrible loss?" I've learned, however, that the balm is applied while we give thanks.

The second exercise was absolute trust that God would heal the gaping and gasping depression in my heart and mind. I equated it with physical surgery; healing finally happens. There are scars, but the pain finally diminishes.

*Thank You, Father! Thank You for delivering me and giving me strength to honor You in the valley of the shadow of my son's death. Thank You! Amen.*

Patricia Erwin Nordman has written numerous articles and meditations. Her booklet on the topic of grief is used world-wide. Besides writing she enjoys reading and working with her computer. She and her husband, Charles, have four sons and make their home in Deland, Florida.

# *Father Knows Best*

**Teresa Olive**

*Show me your ways, O Lord, teach
me your paths; guide me in your
truth and teach me, for you are God
my Savior, and my hope is in you all
day long.* Psalm 25:4-5, *NIV*

We all sighed in relief as we
entered the motel room and felt the icy blast of the
air conditioner. My husband, three children, and I
were feeling the effects of driving cross-country while
crammed into our tiny Toyota. We could hardly wait
for the next day when we would finally reach our
destination—my parents' beach home in North
Carolina.

My husband spread out the road map and called
me over. His voice sounded puzzled. "Look at this,
Terri. Here's the road your dad recommended."

His finger traced the interstate route from
Lexington down to Columbia, South Carolina, then
back up the coast of North Carolina. We exchanged a
bewildered glance. Daddy's way looked at least a

hundred miles longer than the state highway which cut straight through North Carolina.

"Well," I said, "Daddy's lived here most of his life. Maybe he knows something we don't." But the more we thought about that extra mileage, the less Daddy's advice appealed to us.

The next day we decided to follow the state highway. At first we were pleased with our decision. The road was wide and well-paved. However, as we continued, it narrowed and began to climb. As the car rounded one hairpin curve after another, it began to dawn on us—we were in the heart of the Smoky Mountains!

It was almost midnight when we finally pulled up to my parents' home. We had to confess to my father that we hadn't taken his advice and definitely wished that we had.

It struck me then that I often do the same thing with my heavenly Father's advice. It makes sense that the One who designed me knows what is best for me. He has given me His road map to life, the Bible; yet I often ignore it, especially when the way it points seems too hard or inconvenient. I convince myself that my way is better when I'm really just wandering around in circles.

*Father, thank You for the directions You've given me in Your Word. Please help me to follow Your path instead of my own. Amen.*

Teresa Olive is a published writer who enjoys singing, playing piano and guitar, writing songs, and acting in community theater. She and her husband, Jeff, have three daughters and reside in Port Orchard, Washington.

# So What's a Few Blades of Grass?

**Verla E. Oliver**

*Just as a father has compassion on
his children, so the Lord has
compassion on those who fear Him.
For He Himself knows our frame; He
is mindful that we are but dust.*
Psalm 103:13-14, *NASB*

He reminded me of a big, gangly
puppy as he rounded the corner of the school gym.
With his long, suntanned legs, oversized basketball
shoes, and a grin revealing the shine of new braces,
my fourteen-year-old son Matt tossed his backpack
into the car and hopped in. "I want to go fishing this
afternoon, Mom!" he pronounced.

As I pulled out of the parking lot, I thought of the
two fishing trips to the pier he had just made last
week. "Sounds like fun, Matt, but I have some work I

need to finish, and driving you to the pier today won't work out."

He sat thinking. "What if I help you with your work. Then will you have time to drive me to the pier?"

This sounded like a fair offer, so when we arrived home we got started. I washed one half of my dusty car while Matt scrubbed the other half. I cleaned the inside of the windows and Matt polished the outside until they sparkled. Finally, all that was left was the vacuuming.

"I'll vacuum the whole car, Mom," Matt offered generously. "You can go into the house and rest."

When we had finished the remaining chores, I brought a pile of library books out to the car. I opened the door and noticed several yellow blades of grass on the carpet.

*Hmm*, I thought. *Looks like he missed a spot. Oh, there's more grass over there in the corner too.*

My first impulse was to point out to Matt the part of the job that wasn't up to my standard. In my quest for perfection, this is often my first impulse with my children and others. But today I took a deep breath and decided that he had done a good job.

As I walked back into the kitchen, Matt was getting a glass of orange juice out of the refrigerator. "You know, Mom," he said with smile, "I really had fun working with you today."

I gave him a hug and breathed a silent prayer. *Thank You, Lord, for stopping my first impulse.*

We loaded up the fishing gear and drove off towards the pier. As Matt cheerfully described the fish he hoped to catch, I looked down at the carpet and thought, *So what's a few blades of grass?*

*Forgive me, Lord, for my perfectionism, for*

*expectation from myself and others which is only true of You. Thank You for Your compassion on us despite our imperfections. May this compassion be seen in me. Amen.*

Verla E. Oliver, in addition to writing, enjoys aerobics, gardening, walking on the beach, and spending time with her family. In addition, she is a speaker for women's ministries and a volunteer with the American Cancer Society. Verla and her husband, Al, have two children and reside in La Mirada, California.

# God's Perfect Answer

**Patricia L. Opitz**

*Because You have been my help,*
*Therefore in the shadow of Your*
*wings I will rejoice.*
Psalm 63:7, *NKJV*

When Mama had problems she prayed for strength, and God supplied. But this time, she wanted more than strength—she felt she needed human help.

Daddy had kept active after his retirement, until one winter a leg injury put him to bed. While he was down, Mama could handle everything except carrying wood from the yard to the house for their hungry heating stove. Chronic joint pain limited her wood-toting ability to one piece per trip.

During one cold Tuesday morning's devotions, Mama's thoughts drifted to the dwindling woodpile on the porch. She hesitated to pray for a person to help, but then remembered reading Catherine Marshall's account of a prayer for household help. God had sent a woman perfectly suited for the job.

217

Encouraged by Mrs. Marshall's experience, Mama made her request.

Not thirty minutes later, a neighbor, whom my parents knew only slightly, knocked at the back door. He had come to see Daddy, and he visited with him a few minutes. Before he left, he asked Mama if she needed anything. When she told him about the wood, he gladly carried it for her. He even hauled some logs from Daddy's stack ten miles away.

When Mama shared the incident with me, I marveled at our heavenly Father's expression of love. His answer was immediate and specific, as though He had been just waiting for the request.

I wonder how often I've failed to ask when God wants to supply exactly what I need.

*Father, thank You for sending help that perfectly fits my needs. Keep me aware of Your readiness to provide. Amen.*

Patricia L. Opitz is a published writer who enjoys sewing, reading, crocheting, and playing piano. In addition, she is both a public and high school library volunteer. Patricia and her husband, Mike, have one daughter and live in Anadarko, Oklahoma.

# *The Worst Year of My Life*

**Fawn Parish**

*The Lord is near to the brokenhearted, And saves those who are crushed in spirit.*
Psalm 34:18, *NASB*

I never had an ounce of compassion for people who experienced depression. Why couldn't they just master their emotions, for heaven's sake? Didn't they know how their self-pity affected everyone else? What unmitigated selfishness! I was silently merciless. That was, until last year.

No one close to me had died. I hadn't suffered a major illness. We hadn't experienced bankruptcy. In fact, none of the major traumas of life had come our way. Yet, I went through last year like a grief-stricken child. I felt bruised, crushed, and broken.

Everything in my life was in a state of transition. I had left a challenging job to care for my newborn son, but I felt inadequate as a mother. My relationships were changing. I was in a new church that felt strange and unfamiliar. All of my primary sources of affirmation were gone. I couldn't hide behind a nice title on a business card. God was redefining my existence, and He was being painstakingly thorough.

The accusing voice inside me would taunt, "You have no right to feel this way; look at all the things you have to be grateful for." Who could ever argue that? I had a dear husband, a healthy sweet son, a nice home, good health ... the list was endless. Yet inside I ached.

Then one day, unexpectedly, I felt God say He understood my frustrations. He didn't sweep in and change anything. There was no miraculous intervention. Nothing changed except now there was a shared "knowing." He understood and that was enough.

I was amazed at how healing it was to know He understood. I'd forgotten that He was a man of sorrows acquainted with grief. He knew what it was like to be crushed and bruised. He knew the agony of separation from the One who loved Him most. He understood.

I felt affirmed by His understanding. It was comforting to know I wasn't "out to lunch." I wasn't some hormonal basket case. He understood how I felt because He had felt the same way.

As I look back on that horrible year, where every day seemed like six months, I've found something amazing. The year (in retrospect, of course) seems to have been very short. The lessons I've learned—and am still learning—have proven to be invaluable. And, I'm much easier to be around now if you happen to be feeling low.

*Lord, thank You that there is no emotion in life that You have not felt. Thank You for comforting me today with understanding. Because You are near, and because You have felt what I'm feeling, I have hope. Amen.*

Fawn Parish is a writer and speaker who enjoys teaching God's Word, scuba diving, making her own paper, and watching her small son discover the world. She and her husband, Joey, have one child and make their home in Ventura, California.

# A Light Unto
# My Path

**Dalene Vickery Parker**

*Thy word is a lamp unto my feet, and*
*a light unto my path.*
Psalm 119:105, *KJV*

**Q**uiet time is a rare and precious
commodity for the mother of a three-year-old and a
nine-month-old. But I have to have it. That's why I
stay up an hour or so after my husband and children
are in bed so I can read, write, or just muddle
through the day's accomplishments (or lack of) and
set goals for the next day.

When my mind is relaxed enough to let me sleep,
I turn out all the lights in the house and start for
the bedroom. Then, with arms outstretched, I feel my
way down the hall, into our room, around the bed,
until ... Crash! ... Crunch! ... Stumble! ... Bang!!!

"Oh, no, not again," I moan, as I collide with my
son's tricycle and my daughter's musical ball in the
bathroom doorway. Just this morning Daniel and
Susanne played at my feet while I put on my
makeup. Then, when the phone rang at the other

end of the house, we dropped what we were doing and raced to the kitchen. Somehow, I never made my way back to the bedroom until now.

Grumbling inwardly, I nurse my stubbed toe and ask myself for the umpteenth time ... "Why doesn't my husband move the things that might make me fall? Or, more truthfully, why am I not a better housekeeper?" Either solution would solve my problem. Better yet, Pat could leave a light on for me as he does some nights. On the nights he remembers I feel so warm, so protected, so loved. The obstacles may still be there, but in the soft light I can pick my way around them or move them from my path.

It's the same with God sometimes. He doesn't always move obstacles from my path, but He does provide the Light with which I can pick my way through life without falling. Temptation, doubt, and fear are but a few of the roadblocks that may cause me to stumble in the darkness, but God's Word provides the solution for those and any others that obstruct my spiritual path. Best of all, our heavenly Father leaves His light on all the time!

*Thank You, Lord, for the warmth, protection, and love You bestow through the light of Your Holy Word. Help me to use that light to remove the obstacles from my path before they cause me to stumble. Amen.*

Dalene Vickery Parker has authored several poems and articles. In addition she composes the verses for *Glad Tidings*, a greeting card company she co-owns and operates from her home. She and her husband, Pat, have two children and live in Spartanburg, South Carolina.

# When God Whispers

**Margaret Parker**

*Answer me quickly, O Lord; my spirit*
*fails ... .Show me the way I should*
*go, for to you I lift up my soul.*
Psalm 143:7-8, *NIV*

Why won't God tell me plainly
what He wants? Here I am, mired in confusion,
bogged down in indecision, wondering which way to
go next. I pray for guidance, read my Bible, and wait
for an answer. No answer comes. I feel like shouting,
"God, could You please speak up? How am I
supposed to know what You want if You won't tell
me?"

Why, I wonder, does God make Himself so hard to
hear? I almost wish He would bark out clear
commands like some heavenly drill instructor.
Wouldn't that be better than this confusing silence?
On second thought, though, raising His voice might
not be such a good idea. I've tried yelling orders at
my family, and what happens? They tune me out.
Walls go up between us.

A wise parent, I've learned, accomplishes far more by whispering. I can remember a game my father and I played when I was little. He'd beckon to me with a look that said, "Come share a secret." When I drew close, he'd bend down, cup his hand around my ear, and speak very low. Though I listened hard, I couldn't make out the words. But I got the message. Dad wanted me close. His whispering game created intimacy between us.

Perhaps my heavenly Father, too, keeps His voice low because He wants to draw me near Him. As I lean closer to hear, gradually I recognize His whisper in the smallest things, in a friend's touch, an uneasy feeling inside me, a snatch of conversation, or a line from a book. The messages are not loud or sharp, and I can't be sure I've heard His directions correctly, but as I learn to quiet myself and listen I get something better than answers. God gives me Himself. His presence becomes real and personal, as real as a warm hand cupped against my cheek, as personal as a secret whispered in my ear.

*Heavenly Father, when I feel confused and unsure what direction I should take, help me experience Your presence and rest in Your love. Amen.*

Margaret Parker has authored a book, Unlocking the Power of God's Word, as well as a variety of articles, meditations, Sunday School curriculum, and leaders' guides. In addition, she leads the Diablo Valley Christian Writers' Group. Margaret and her husband, Bill, have one daughter and reside in Walnut Creek, California.

# Shade and Shadows

**Shirley R. Pease**

*The Lord watches over you, the Lord
is your shade at your right hand.*
Psalm 121:5, *NIV*

Grief wrapped its fingers around
my heart, for now, after forty years of marriage, my
husband had begun his eternity.

I hugged my Bible to my breast and rocked and
rocked in my chair. The sun's reflection through the
window warmed my body, but my heart was cold. I
struggled to write my feelings in my journal.

Through tears my scribblings were jumbled and
confusing. Just as I began to spew out my anger on
the white page, I noticed the shadow under my right
hand. It followed closely underneath. As though
spoken aloud, the words from the Psalm rushed
through my head. "The Lord is the shade at your
right hand."

Suddenly, the spell of despair was broken, and I
knew I was not alone. For the first time peace spilled
over me like a soft cloud wrapping me in love. My

heart laid bare by the rawness of separation gave way to the truth of God's Word.

Sometimes I am still lonely, but I know I am never alone. God is as close to me as the shadow on the written page. And He's with me all day long and through the night.

*Father, thank You for Your peace and the truth of Your Word. Please help me to remember in my times of loneliness just how close You really are. Amen.*

Shirley R. Pease is a free-lance writer who enjoys reading, walking, and growing African violets. Shirley has five married children and makes her home in East Wenatchee, Washington.

# Door Holder

**Cora Lee Pless**

*Better is one day in your courts than
a thousand elsewhere; I would rather
be a doorkeeper in the house of my
God than dwell in the tents of the
wicked.* Psalm 84:10, *NIV*

Several years ago my son and
daughter frequently argued about who was going to
be first to do or to receive something. In exasperation
I would remind them, "The Bible says, 'The last shall
be first, and the first last.'"

That usually confused them enough to stop the
arguing for the moment, but before long they would
be at it again.

Then, one night during family devotions, my
husband read the Scripture from Matthew 20:16 that
ended with the now-famous verse.

"See," I exclaimed, "I told you the Bible says, 'The
last shall be first, and the first last'!"

"Sure, Mom," my son said nonchalantly, "it's like
being door holder. You're the first one to the door but
then you hold it for everyone else, so then you're
last."

Mentally, I pictured my son's kindergarten class.
Each time the class lined up to go somewhere, the
child designated as door holder would take his place

at the front of the line. Then, when the class reached a door, the door holder would step aside and hold the door open for the rest of the class to pass through. After everyone had gone through the door, the door holder again would take his place in line. Only now, instead of being first in line, the door holder would be last.

The door holder gave up his position as first in order to be of service to others and then found himself last. This evidently made an impression on my son. It also made an impression on me.

Often I think about the door holder when I find myself seeking to be first. Of course, I never openly argue with others about being first. But sometimes I prefer to do the work that brings praise, to hold the offices that bring recognition, to perform the important tasks. Sometimes I become jealous when others gain positions of honor.

Then I remember that God asks me to be more like a door holder, to give up my apparent right to be first, in order to be of service, even if it means being last. That means to work even when someone else receives the credit, to help others even when I receive no honor or praise. In other words, I try to accept with humility and with gladness the position of door holder.

*Dear Lord, may I humbly serve You by helping others. Help me to hold a door for someone today. Amen.*

Cora Lee Pless has written numerous articles. In addition, she enjoys teaching adult Sunday School classes, playing the piano, reading, gardening, and doing handwork. Cora Lee and her husband, Chuck, have one daughter and one son and reside in Mooresville, North Carolina.

# A Gift From the "Guys"

**Darlene Rose Pritchard**

*The Lord sustains all who fall, and
raises up all who are bowed down.*
Psalm 145:14, *NASB*

It all happened so quickly! Down
on the ice, crutches flying! What a way to end a
special Christmas trip to California. In his usual
good humor, David, my husband, was laughing. Dave
Jr. and George in chorus were laughing and saying,
"Do it again, Dad, that was neat!" I was immediately
afraid, but the fear was short-lived as he got up and
brushed off the snow and drove us home.

One week later while visiting with friends and
watching the Super Bowl, David quietly said to me,
"Honey, you know when I fell last week and landed
on my left elbow; I think it's starting to swell up. It's
beginning to hurt a lot." A trip to the doctor the next
morning confirmed a break in the ball of the elbow.
For me, a broken arm would be an annoying six
weeks, but for David a broken arm is a major event.
David is a triple amputee. His left arm is used for
everything. Without his arm he can't walk, eat,
drive, or go to work.

As I lay awake that first night, my heart was paralyzed with fear and my mind was filled with questions. *There's no sick leave with this job; how will we make it? We just used up a lot of vacation time; is there enough vacation time left for his arm to heal? If it takes longer, how will we pay the bills?*

Eventually David's vacation time was used up, and finances were getting tight. I had been encouraged time after time as food appeared on the doorstep: eggs, carrots, potatoes, milk, and prepared meals. Yet, I lay awake nights worrying and asking the Lord, "What about the house payment, the electric bill, the phone bill, the doctor bill, the insurance?"

Never will I forget the night the doorbell rang and a friend of David's from work came to visit. She laid a large manila envelope on the couch next to him. She stayed awhile; then as she left she said, "This is a little something the guys wanted you to have." I sat on the couch with David and we looked with amazement at the money fluttering out of the envelope. Later I counted it, then counted it again. We looked at each other, amazed to find that the gift from the "guys" was just what David's next paycheck would have been.

*O Lord, You remind me again and again of Your presence. Thank You for sustaining me when I fall and raising me up when I falter under the unexpected events of my life. Amen.*

Darlene Rose Pritchard enjoys reading, writing poetry, bird-watching, crocheting, collecting antiques, and teaching Sunday School. She and her husband, David, have two sons and make their home in Emmett, Idaho.

# Parable of the Hearth

**Colleen L. Reece**

*Your word is a lamp to my feet and a
light for my path.*
Psalm 119:105, *NIV*

And it came to pass that a decree
went out that all must prepare their homes, for the
Master was coming. Every hovel, hut, and palace
must be swept, polished, and decorated, for in the
household that showed the greatest care and love
would the Master abide.

It also came to pass that three good women lived
near one another—one in a palace, one in a sturdy
house, and the third in a small hut. Each greeted the
decree according to her situation.

"My!" the princess in the palace, who had taken
over on the death of her mother the queen, sighed.
"Never has there been such an honor. Come!" She
clapped her hands sharply and many servants came
running. "We have much to do ere the Master
comes."

The second woman had no servants, but she set

to work scrubbing and polishing, heart beating fast over the Master's visit.

The little woman in the hut had no need to scrub or polish. Her small abode always shone with loving care. So she started preparing the single thing she had to honor her Master.

And it came to pass that the Master, dusty and worn, came to the palace. The servants had wrought well. The princess clapped her hands with joy when the Master said, "I will stay with you a night and a day, for the sake of your servants' work."

At the second home the Master smiled. "Thank you for your preparations. I will rest with you two nights and two days." He went on, leaving his hostess-to-be grateful and happy.

Weary and footsore, the Master reached the tiny hut. His keen eyes sought out every corner and at last rested on the only preparation the little woman could make other than a small cake and a little broth. A crude candle, fashioned from hoarded tallow drippings of many stubs, lighted the room.

"Good sister," the Master said. "Will you not be in darkness once I have gone? You have used all you have to welcome me."

The little woman shook her head. "Nay, Master. The light of Your Presence will brighten my hut until the end of my days."

"And beyond," the Master told her. "Because you have given with graciousness what you have, here will I stay once the three days and three nights I have promised end."

At one time I envied others their possessions. The Lord loved and guided my thinking into higher paths. I now know He wants the gracious giving of all I have—and am. Like the little woman, the light of God's presence brightens all my days.

*Dear Lord, may I ever offer my all and my best, even when that best is humble. The Son-light of Your Word truly is a lamp to guide me. Amen.*

Colleen L. Reece is a full-time writer/teacher/lecturer and the author of *The Workbook Way: Writing Smarter, Not Harder*, (Evergreen, 1992). Besides writing Colleen enjoys reading, working in her church, and yardwork. She makes her home in Auburn, Washington.

# I Will Rejoice ... In the Morning?

**Mary-Anne Reed**

*This is the day the Lord has made;*
*let us rejoice and be glad in it.*
Psalm 118:24, *NIV*

The words *groggy* and *cranky* used to describe how I felt when I first woke up in the morning. While my husband sprang out of bed with a cheerful grin on his face every morning at five, it was all I could do to muster up enough strength to pull myself out of a prone position two hours later; I wasn't a lot of fun to be around.

I continued to believe that people's moods were just naturally different, like Snow White's dwarfs: In the morning some can't help being "Dopey" and "Grumpy," while others are "Happy" and whistle while they work throughout the day.

Then one day I asked my husband why he was so *alive* in the morning. He explained: "When I open my eyes, the first thing I say to myself is: 'This is the day the Lord has made, I will rejoice and be glad in it.' After that, I start smiling!"

Was it really that simple?

The next morning, feeling like I had been drugged with a thousand tranquilizers, I tried it. Eyes half opened, I propped myself up on one elbow, leaned against my pillow, and mumbled a prayer: "Okay, Lord, I'll give it a try, even though I don't feel like rejoicing."

Then I repeated the Scripture out loud: "This is the day that the Lord has made. I will rejoice and be glad in it." My voice was cracking and anyone within earshot wouldn't have believed me.

I tried it again. And this time as I spoke the words, my vocal cords heavy laden with sleep began clearing, my eyes cranked fully open and I felt … How did I feel? No I didn't feel cheerful, but I did feel better. In some small way, my mood had been affected. I began to theorize: *What if I practiced rejoicing and impressing my mind with God's Word throughout the day. What kind of spiritual giant might I become?* Then it suddenly hit me: Many of the great Christian heroes and heroines I had read about practiced this kind of continual dwelling on and rejoicing in God's Word.

Ever since I began putting this idea into practice a few years ago, even my husband will admit that mornings have improved greatly around our house. What's even better, my attitude has become more joyful, reflecting the Good News of God's Word.

*Lord, help me to commit myself to dwelling on Your eternal message of great hope throughout my day. Keep me from unnecessary and harmful distractions. Inspire me to focus on Your truth. Amen.*

Mary-Anne Reed is a free-lance writer and editor and has written several articles for magazines and newspapers. She enjoys reading, jogging, traveling, sports, and music. Mary-Anne and her husband make their home in Ojai, California.

# *Just Like King David*

**Lei Loni Rodrigues**

*But I have trusted in Thy lovingkindness; My heart shall rejoice in Thy salvation.* Psalm 13:5, *NASB*

As I read God's Word, the inspiration is overwhelming, especially this morning. It's quiet, the kids are still asleep, and I feel inspired by the writings of King David in the Psalms.

The joys of being the proud mother of two healthy, full-of-life, seldom satisfied kids can sometimes be overshadowed by the fears of being a single parent raising two healthy, full-of-life, seldom satisfied kids.

Being the primary and only decision maker is an awesome responsibility. Suppose I make a mistake—a wrong decision concerning their needs? Suppose I'm too liberal—or too strict! And what if I squelch their creativity and, thereby, ruin them for life? Oh, my dear Lord!

Even though I'm a woman, I identify with King David. I hear myself in his cries to the Lord.

David speaks of his enemies and his fears. While I don't have human enemies, none that I know of anyway, I do have a myriad of spiritual enemies constantly trying to destroy my spirit. Enemies, like fear, frustration, worry, doubt, loneliness, anger, lust, jealousy, greed, and deceit, lurk, as David says in Psalm 10:9: "He lurks in a hiding place as a lion in a lair; He lurks to catch the afflicted." This is exactly how I envision those tireless and tenacious terrors.

In Psalm 13:1-3, David cries to the Lord, "How long, Oh Lord? Wilt Thou forget me forever? ... How long shall I take counsel in my soul, having sorrow in my heart all the day? How long will my enemy be exalted over me?"

Sometimes my fear is so great that, just like King David, I wonder if God has forgotten about me. Yet, like David, at the end of my cries I can say, "But I have trusted in Thy lovingkindness; My heart shall rejoice in Thy salvation. I will sing to the Lord, because He has dealt bountifully with me" (Psalm 13:5).

*Lord, I will sing to You and my heart shall rejoice in Thy salvation. I know that just as You delivered King David from the hands of his enemies, so shall You deliver me. Thank You, Lord. Amen.*

Lei Loni Rodrigues is a single mom who besides working full-time outside of her home enjoys writing, reading, and singing. She and her two children make their home in Hayward, California.

# The Sweetest Burden

**Susan S. Rogers**

*Cast thy burden upon the Lord, and
he shall sustain thee: he shall never
suffer the righteous to be moved.*
Psalm 55:22, *KJV*

This afternoon as my daughter
and I were driving home from the Mother's Morning
Out program, she fell asleep, exhausted from several
hours of active playtime. When we turned into our
driveway, I was thinking of the many packages I
would have to carry into the house in addition to a
thirty-pound toddler.

I reached across the seat for her, and, even in
deep sleep, she instinctively placed her head on my
shoulder and her arms over my back. It was difficult
manuevering her out of the car and around the
steering wheel. I almost groaned from the burden of
supporting her weight and from the awkwardness of
my position. Then, as she settled her head onto my
shoulder, I heard her faintly call out, "Mama," before
drifting into trusted restfulness.

As I carried her up the stairway, her hair damp and tousled, her little hands moist, and her barrettes loosened, I looked into her cherubic face and thought, *This is the sweetest burden I'll ever carry*. In the same moment I was feeling overwhelmed by the most unqualified love that I will likely ever know.

I thought of how at times I may feel weary with life's burdens: unhappiness, despair, unpleasantness in the home or work place, the death of a loved one, the responsibility for an aging parent, the loss of a friend's goodwill, or some other misfortune. Sometimes when the load seems too crushing, I take comfort in knowing that there is a higher power giving me strength to bear it.

*Dear God, thank You for caring for me. When I am toiling under a heavy weight, please let me feel Your presence beside me. Help me to carry on when sometimes my mission is unclear or filled with obstructions. Amen.*

Susan S. Rogers, in addition to writing, enjoys collecting cookbooks and trying new recipes, and attending craft and hobby shows. She and her husband, Jack, have one daughter and make their home in Rome, Georgia.

# *Too Late Smart?*

**Barbara Rouleau**

*Teach me your way, O Lord, and I will walk in your truth; give me an undivided heart, that I may fear your name.* Psalm 86:11, *NIV*

While gift shopping with my friend Essie, we paused at a display of kitchenware and household whimsies. She picked up a small plaque decorated with the legend, "We Grow Too Soon Old, Too Late Smart."

Ruefully, she put it down as we smiled knowingly at each other and quickly passed it by. We didn't need such a reminder of the years told by our graying hair. But that oft repeated adage stayed with me that day, needling me again and again.

Although a Christian for many years, had I grown old too soon, smart too late? How could I have lived so long under the banner of Christ and still conformed so poorly to the image of God's only begotten Son? My judgment of myself tends to be severe.

Then I read again Psalm 86. In his commentary, Matthew Henry writes: "We cannot walk in God's way and truth unless He teach us; and if we expect He should teach us we must resolve to be governed by His teachings."

Like many Christians I have acknowledged Christ and learned of His truth. But in many subtle little ways I have resisted His teachings, lacked the resolve to be governed by His way. A positive, active determination to be governed by His way is the attitude He wants from me.

On my own, I am weak and often fail. But if I'm diligent in seeking to do His will, He will always meet my need. I have this glorious assurance expressed by the apostle Paul: "Being confident of this, that he who began a good work in you will carry it on to completion until the day of Christ Jesus" (Philippians 1:6).

Too soon old, too late smart? It's never too late, while there is life and breath, to seek Him, to learn of Him, and to walk in His truth!

*Father, give me an undivided heart. Help me to be faithful and diligent to follow Jesus as You reveal Your will for me by Your Word and Holy Spirit. Amen.*

Barbara Rouleau is a published writer who also enjoys reading, traveling, cooking, crocheting, and being with her family. She and her husband, Arthur, have one daughter with whom they make their home in Garden Grove, California.

# Freedom From Fear

**Cherie L. Rouleau**

*I sought the Lord, and He heard me,*
*And delivered me from all my fears."*
Psalm 34:4, *NKJV*

A few days before my
hysterectomy, I learned that the suspect cyst on my
ovary was probably cancer. My first reaction was, "I
don't want to go through what David did."

Twelve years earlier I watched my brother die,
his body ravaged by numerous cancers and the
results of chemotherapy treatments. Doctors dangled
what I construed to be ridiculous medical carrots in
front of him. It seemed they were more interested in
using him for experimentation than maintaining the
quality of his last year of life.

Now, I too faced the dreaded big "C."

I clung to a verse given to me years before by my
pastor when I was caught up with other fears. "For
God has not given us a spirit of fear, but of power
and of love and of a sound mind" (2 Timothy 1:7).

Through the following weeks, I faced good news

and bad, still holding tight to my verse. The good news: "We think we got it all with surgery." The bad news: "We'll have to wait for pathology for the final determination." The good news: "We think it was stage one." The bad news: "You should probably undergo chemotherapy."

The night before the doctor's appointment that would give me the final pathology report and chemotherapy projection, I lay in bed, a dark cloud of speculation hanging over me. "Should I buy wigs now?" "Will I be able to work?" "Where do I want to be buried?"

Finally, in desperation, I cried, "Lord, I don't care what I have to face as long as You'll take the fear away. With You I can face anything, even death." Immediately peace enveloped me.

I still have most of my five years of careful watching before I am declared cured. But now I sing with the Psalmist, "I sought the Lord, and he heard me, And delivered me from all my fears."

*Thank You, Lord, for release from fear, and for freedom to have Your power and love envelope me. Thank You for the gift of a sound mind. Amen.*

Cherie L. Rouleau is a published poet. She is a secretary who in her spare time enjoys writing, music, and ceramics. Cherie makes her home in Garden Grove, California.

# Thanks for
# Being There

**Jane Rumph**

*Trust in him at all times, O people;
pour out your hearts to him, for God
is our refuge.* Psalm 62:8, *NIV*

I need to talk to someone," the
caller began. "I ... I just feel like killing myself!" she
blurted, bursting into tears.

As a volunteer on a Christian telephone help line,
I recognized the despair in the caller's voice.
Hesitantly, she started sharing her troubles—a failed
relationship with a man, a fractured job history,
estrangement from her family.

I listened quietly, from time to time trying
carefully to reflect empathy and understanding of
her feelings. As the call progressed I could hear her
voice calming. She began to open up and express
herself more freely as she described her situation to
the anonymous listening ear on my end of the line.

Thirty minutes passed. I had said very little
when the caller, sounding much more composed,
sighed and said, "You know, I feel better just talking

246

with you. Thanks for being there."

As we hung up, I smiled and reflected on how many times this had happened over my years at the help line. Distressed callers, with no one else to turn to, frequently want nothing more than to pour out their hearts to someone who will listen confidentially and compassionately without interruption, advice, or judgment.

I said a quick prayer of thanks for the family and friends I can talk to when I need someone to understand. And as I did so I realized afresh how precious it is to have God Himself ready at all times to sit down with me and listen to all that is on my heart. How wonderful that I can trust my heavenly Father not only to accept me unconditionally but to provide a safe place in which to rediscover His peace and presence.

"Thanks for being there, Lord," I whispered. I turned to do my paperwork, and the phone rang again.

"Hello? I need somebody to talk to ... ."

*Dear Father, You never fail to hear me when I pour out my heart to You. Empower me to give others that same refuge by loving and listening as You do. Amen.*

Jane Rumph is a free-lance writer who has published numerous articles and devotions. In addition, she enjoys reading, baking, traveling, and playing piano, flute, and piccolo. Jane and her husband, Dave, reside in Pasadena, California.

# Joy Around the Corner

**Margaret Sampson**

*Direct me in the path of your
commands, for there I find delight.*
Psalm 119:35, *NIV*

I stopped. The woods became
suddenly quiet without the melodic swish-swish of
my cross-country skis. The path I had followed uphill
for the past mile bent steeply down in front of me,
then turned a corner. *Will there be enough room after
this curve to slow down for the next one?* I wondered.
If I fell, my old spinal injury might act up again.
Maybe I would be wise to turn back, but I couldn't
pry myself from the lovely vista ahead.

I looked down at the smooth ski tracks, the
testimony of many adventurers who had gone before
me. Not a single ski had strayed to cut the snow
outside the two grooves. No sitzmarks—the holes
that fallen skiers leave behind—showed in the white
banks.

I held my breath and let the tracks lead my skis
around the bend. The slope treated me to a roller
coaster thrill through dense evergreens. Then the
trail opened straight before me again, and I skied
with new vigor.

This experience reminded me of another safe plunge I had taken as a new Christian. I worked in a government agency, where the other economists were reserved about their religion. Shy to begin with, I felt discouraged and unsure about witnessing.

Cybil seemed even more shy. When I saw her in the hall, she walked with her head down. I heard from a colleague that she attended church.

In my home Bible study for career women, I had learned that we Christians are commanded to encourage each other. My study leader coached me, showing me how she had started our group. It sounded simple.

One day I decided to trust in God and follow my study leader's example. When I saw Cybil in the hall, I said hello and asked her if she would join me for lunch. She was reserved at first, but after I told her that I went to church, too, and believed and followed Christ, she became a sister. We discovered we were both single, with similar struggles at work.

After that day, Cybil's face lit up every time we met. We agreed to have lunch together once a week. Before long, more women joined us to study the Bible and pray for each other.

As it was on that snowy hill, joy was just around that scary corner of the first hello.

*Dear Lord, I trust in You when I can't see around the corner. When I step out in Your will, wonderful things lie ahead. Help me take that first step. Amen.*

Margaret Sampson is a full-time writer who enjoys skiing, hiking, traveling, and nursing home and evangelism ministry. In addition, she is a ski instructor for a Christian ski school. Margaret makes her home in Kirkland, Washington.

# Between a Dog and a Hard Place

**Dee Sand**

*I will say of the Lord, "He is my
refuge and my fortress, my God, in
whom I trust." Surely He will save
you from the fowler's snare and from
the deadly pestilence.*
Psalm 91:2-3, *NIV*

The library is closing. Do you want
to check out that book?" The librarian's voice jolted
me back to reality.

As I gazed at the first stars appearing in the
evening sky, I knew it was not safe for a thirteen-
year-old girl to walk the streets alone after dark. But
now I had no choice. With home a half a mile away, I
started out, eyes forward, briskly putting one foot in
front of the other.

When I was two blocks from the library, a dark
blue car slowed to a crawl beside me. The leering

expression on the driver's face turned my apprehension to terror. "Hop in, Honey, I'll take you home."

"No, thanks, I'm almost home," I answered. Then I crossed the street. *Please, Lord*, I prayed, *please get me home safely*.

Before long the same blue car came from the other direction. I looked up and down the street for a house with lights on, but saw none. *Please, God, not this*. Again I crossed to the other side of the street.

The car pulled away only to circle the block a third time. *God, if You don't save me now, I'll never get home*, I prayed as I saw the car again.

Just then I heard a deep snarling growl. A huge white dog came out from between two houses and bounded toward me. He ran full force, barking and baring his teeth. Now I was caught between a dog and a hard place. From where would my deliverance come? The car slowed; the dog didn't. Which would be the worse danger?

Soon the man in the car drove away; I froze in terror. Miraculously this barking, snarling monster came to a halt and sat at my feet. I took a step; the dog got up. I turned and slowly walked away; the dog trotted at my side. At the corner, he sat at my feet until the light turned green and I stepped off the curb.

This huge white dog walked me to my front door, barked once, and bounded away, never to be seen again.

The Lord told Isaiah, "My thoughts are not your thoughts, neither are your ways my ways" (55:8). I know my Lord cares for me and hears my prayers. And though my deliverance came from an unexpected place, there is no doubt that God, Himself, intervened to rescue me from the fowler's snare.

*Dear Father, how many times have I failed to see Your hand because my ways are not Your ways? Thank You for loving and answering the prayers of Your children. Amen.*

Dee Sand is a storyteller turned writer. She has written and performed dramatic monologues portraying biblical characters for several years. She enjoys baking bread and needlework. Dee and her husband, Kevin, have two children and make their home in Philadelphia, Pennsylvania.

# Gems of Joy

**Joyce E. Schmedel**

*His favor lasts a lifetime; weeping*
*may remain for a night, but rejoicing*
*comes in the morning.*
Psalm 30:5, *NIV*

The antiseptic hospital corridors
intensified my loneliness as I walked away from my
Dad's room. Tears marked my face. I recalled the
chalky blue appearance lung cancer made on his
oxygen starved body, leaving him pale and
breathless. As my feet mechanically moved to the
elevator, I knew I had said good-bye for the last
time. Turning, I waved to him forcing a smile. He
lifted a weary hand to wave back as our eyes met.
He knew it too.

In bed that night I sobbed my prayerful grief,
cradled in the arms of my heavenly Father. Unable
to sleep, I turned on a light and opened my Bible.
Slowly turning the pages, my eyes caught the
phrase, "Weeping may remain for a night but
rejoicing comes in the morning." Searching for
comfort, I devoured Psalm 30. Verse 2 spoke of
healing. Was God going to do a miracle? Peace

flooded my heart at the possibility.

I awoke to the sun breaking the horizon. When I began reminding God that joy was to come in the morning, the telephone interrupted.

"Joyce, I'm calling from the hospital to inform you that your dad died a half hour ago. He slipped away with a peaceful smile on his face."

My soul wailed, "Oh, God. I thought You would heal him. This is not the joy You promised."

For hours I struggled with God's harsh, twisted sense of humor as I made necessary phone calls and arrangements. That afternoon I returned to the hospital to pick up my dad's belongings. Nurses gathered around me to express sympathy.

"Your dad was such a wonderful man!"

"Everyone who met him loved him."

"He was quite a Christian, wasn't he? I found him praying in the middle of the night, and he said his life was in God's merciful hands."

I gasped. My heart soared with joy. For years I had prayed for my dad's salvation, left books, and dropped hints all to no outward avail. One week before he died, I confronted him with the need for a decision for Christ. We prayed together and he invited Christ into his heart. I'd hoped it was sincere.

Now I knew it was. The rejoicing of the morning was my dad's: an assured salvation and an immediate presence with the Lord. There was joy for me as well: that God's favor is truly for a lifetime— an eternal lifetime.

*I praise You, Lord, for helping me see the eternal perspective of answered prayer. Thank You for preparing me for those traumatic circumstances that would devastate me if it were not for those gems of joy*

*You drop into my heart when I need them most. Amen.*

Joyce E. Schmedel has written articles, devotions, Sunday School plays, and a juvenile fiction series to be published by Evergreen in 1992. She enjoys teaching Bible studies, drawing and painting, reading, and sewing. Joyce and her husband, John, have one son and one daughter and reside in Camarillo, California.

# Be Still and Know

**Wanda J. Scott**

*Be still, and know that I am God; I
will be exalted among the nations, I
will be exalted in the earth.*
Psalm 46:10, *NIV*

All my activity and all my
busyness seem so fruitless. My quiet time and prayer
life are crowded out with a list of insignificant things
to accomplish each day, and always my list seems to
outlast the day.

I throw a load of laundry into the washing
machine, then wash the breakfast dishes. Next I run
the sweeper and vow that if there are no phone calls
or unexpected interruptions I will jot a note to my
mother. I might even get in an hour of writing before
the invasion of starving teenagers, who have
developed sinus problems from always having their
heads in the refrigerator.

One morning, as I checked my list, that still
small voice within me said, "Be still, and know that I
am God. You race from one project to another, always

trying to finish one so you can jump right into the next. You never take time to enjoy anything you do."

Stopping for a moment, I reflected on what I had just heard. *It's true*, I thought, *there is no joy in anything I do lately. My body is weary, and I've lost my inner peace.* "Yes, Lord," I said. "I will be still and listen for Your voice. I will be still and rest in You. I will wait patiently for You and lean upon You."

I determined to develop a sensitive spirit, one that would allow me to discern what really needs to be done in a day and what are selfish demands on my time. I determined to rest in the Lord, wait patiently for Him, and lean upon Him always.

*I exalt You O Lord. Help me to make my time profitable unto You. Restore unto me the joy of Thy salvation. Amen.*

Wanda J. Scott has written one book and numerous articles for magazines, newspapers, and newsletters. She enjoys reading and playing tennis. Wanda and her husband own a bookstore and have the Solid Rock Ministries. The Scotts have four children and reside in Wheeling, West Virginia.

# Those Baby Monitors!

**Beth Donigan Seversen**

*I will say to the Lord, "My refuge and my fortress, my God, in whom I trust!"* Psalm 91:2, *NASB*

Kate, my ten-day-old daughter, was asleep in her crib on the second floor of our small Cape Cod home. I had neglected to ask my husband to instruct me in the use of our new baby monitor and was certain it was quite beyond me. "What did mothers do before the invention of baby monitors?" I asked myself as I ironed in the basement.

The OBGYN had given me strict instructions due to the trauma of Kate's birth, "One trip up and down the stairs a day, for two weeks!" Yet there I was, running up two flights of stairs after each garment I ironed. Once there I leaned breathlessly over the crib rail to assure myself that my helpless little babe was still breathing. On the trip back to the basement I would scold myself harshly for being so silly. But, once again, while I was bending over the ironing board, fearful thoughts relentlessly teased, *What if crib death steals my baby away, or what if she chokes and I'm not there to help her?* So, back up the stairs I trod.

After one of those completed round trips, the question I'd asked earlier interrupted my fretting. *What did mothers do before baby monitors?* The still small voice residing in my heart replied, "They trusted in the Lord far more, worried far less, and got a lot more accomplished!"

Soon my thoughts were drawn to Matthew 6:25,27: "Therefore I tell you, do not worry about your life ... Who of you by worrying can add a single hour to his life?" (*NIV*). I knew then it was time to pause and confess:

*Thank You, Father, that little Kate is of great value to You and that she is under Your constant watch. I am ashamed of my worries. Please forgive me and help me to trust her life to You always. Amen.*


Beth Donigan Seversen is an associate pastor of women's ministries, supervising Bible studies and programs for working women and moms of preschoolers. A published writer, she enjoys playing golf, entertaining, machine quilting, and water aerobics. The Seversens have two children and reside in Wauwatosa, Wisconsin.

# Thanks for Nothing

**Jessica Shaver**

*Enter His gates with thanksgiving,*
*And his courts with praise.*
Psalm 100:4, *NASB*

**M**y brother once said that the trouble with being an atheist is that when your motorcycle plunges off a cliff into the Colorado River and you aren't killed, there's no one to thank. I'm not an atheist, but sometimes I forget to thank God for the things that haven't happened.

I want to thank Him now for accidents I wasn't involved in, illnesses that never developed, and times I could have been mugged but wasn't. I'm grateful our house didn't burn down when I left the iron on all night. I thank God that our neighbors found the convicted rapist outside our bathroom window before he could get into the house. I'm thankful for every phone call in the middle of the night that is a wrong number and not a death in the family.

Although living on one of the world's most dangerous earthquake faults, I thank God we don't have to worry much about avalanches, tornadoes, volcanoes, mud slides, or floods.

I'm glad our cat survived getting her head caught

in the mayonnaise jar, and I'm glad I know a missionary in Colombia who was bitten by a piranha—so I have something to talk about.

I thank God for all the times I've tripped over my son's book bag or couldn't find a place for the margarine in the fridge door because that's where my daughter keeps her nail polish; these remind me that I have a family. I'm thankful for the night the baby wouldn't let me sleep, when his sobs finally quieted, my exasperation turned to peace, and we rocked sleepily together in the moonlight, his downy head against my cheek.

A friend once told me that nine of her laborsaving devices were broken. Until last year, I didn't even have nine laborsaving devices. So even when they're broken, I'm thankful I have them at all.

Sometimes I forget to thank God for electricity, but now I want to make a point of it. I'm also thankful for indoor plumbing, anesthetics and especially for paper products. Ever since our daughter sheared off the tip of her finger in the bathroom door, I'm thankful for every uneventful day.

I appreciate our small son's paraphrase of Psalm 100: "Enter into his gates on Thanksgiving." I'm glad I have Someone to thank.

*Lord, I want to thank You ahead of time for what You will reveal to us when we see You—how many disasters we don't even know about that You are protecting us from. Amen.*

Jessica Shaver free-lances for newspapers and Christian family magazines. She and her husband have a son and daughter and live in Long Beach, California. ("Thanks for Nothing" first appeared in *Moody Monthly*, November 1988.)

# Hit by a Car

**Pauline Sheehan**

*Even in darkness light dawns for the
upright, for the gracious and
compassionate and righteous man.*
Psalm 112:4, *NIV*

Sharon's been hit by a car. Come
to Elm and Third."

The phone call froze my thoughts like the still
frame of a movie. My actions became deliberate as
the movie continued in slow motion.

I grabbed my purse, left a note, walked to the car,
put the key in the ignition, shifted. I proceeded,
stopped at a stop sign, looked both ways, arrived at
the accident scene, set the parking brake.

Each sweep of the emergency vehicle lights
revealed more of the wreckage. I heard her cry, then
spotted her jackknifed in the ditch. Branches tangled
her hair and tears smeared her face. I caressed her
and wiped her hair from her face, but I couldn't take
away the terror in her eyes.

She groaned through an ambulance ride, X rays,
lab tests, and physical examinations.

Hours later, I took her one-year-old child home

with me, wrapped him in his grandfather's T-shirt, and laid him beside me. In this crisis-filled night, it would just have to do.

He cried and refused his bottle. I patted him, hugged him, and readjusted the covers. How could I console him? How would I explain a drunk driver to a baby? It seemed unfair to me too.

I clenched my fists and argued with God for both of us. "Thrown off the headlight, plowed under the car, dragged in the ditch! God, You were there. You saw the drunk. I hate the driver. I hate our laws. God, let me hate a little longer." Of course, this didn't help us sleep.

Sleep deprived and enraged, I finally asked God. "What do You have for me so that we can get some sleep?"

Only after I was honest with God, did I remember the Psalm that said that light dawns even in the darkest calamity. I breathed deeply, trying to really believe that promise, for the calamity loomed larger than the light.

"God, You gave Your promise; help me believe it."

As soon as I prayed, I felt as if God wrapped his arms around us. Both of us relaxed and fell asleep.

*God, help me remember Your encouragement, for You are with me during the darkest calamity. Amen.*

Pauline J. Sheehan has published numerous articles, poems, stories, cartoons, and devotions. Besides writing she enjoys playing the Omnicord and harp, taking walks, and crocheting. Pauline resides in Lake Stevens, Washington.

# Psalms of Pain

**Elona Peters Siemsen**

*Give ear to my words, O Lord,
consider my groaning. Heed the
sound of my cry for help, my King
and my God.* Psalm 5:1-2, *NASB*

Some of our psalms are melodies of joy. Some are from a heart of pain.

She told me her story. I listened, stunned. The terrible scenes swirled through my head like silent screams. Such things don't happen to people I know. Such things should never happen to anyone. And never, ever, to a child.

But they happened to a child. To the child my friend once was, the child that still lived, trembling, within her mind.

Until now, in discussions with people about the tragedies in this world, I've probably said something like "That's terrible. But we all suffer, and it passes. We need to pray hard and move on. Oh, could you pass the creamer, please?"

I felt fairly content with my little packages of life. That's when I saw mostly the neat side, the finished seams. That's before I saw the torn, ragged edges, the raw side of suffering.

That's before I sat down with a friend and heard her story, unscrubbed, unsanitized, as she lived it, as she is living it now. Miraculously, I finally, *finally* opened my ears and shut my mouth and let a person say what she meant and feel what she felt.

Somehow, I let myself feel what I felt too. As she talked, I felt shock, rage, despair. I wept. I felt her agonized questions and some of my own. And then I felt guilt because of my questions. It was a while later that I realized the Lord of the Universe can handle any questions, any feelings I come up with—the ones that are unscrubbed, unjoyful. I am told that by the Psalms. And by Gethsemane.

I am told I have an Eternal Father who listens. The answers to questions may be afar off for a long time, but the listening heart is here now.

My friend has deeply touched me with her honesty and her courage. More, in trusting me with her most painful secrets, she has given me the gift of herself. I hold that gift tenderly and with awe. I wish I could give her the gift of answers. I cannot. But I will try to give her a listening heart. I will cry with her. And when she feels her psalm of joy will never come, I will keep listening for its far-off strains.

*O Father, You have always listened to me, tenderly and without condemnation. In that same way, help me listen to others. Help me be a friend who shares the psalms of joy and the psalms of pain. Amen.*

Elona Peters Siemsen is a published writer who enjoys reading, painting, singing, writing songs, gardening, animals, and calligraphy. Elona and her husband, Armon, have three grown children and make their home in Whittier, California.

# Freed From the Raging Waters

**Analie Smith**

*Your path led through the sea, your
way through the mighty waters,
though your footprints were not seen.*
Psalm 77:19 *NIV*

The raging waters threatened to
engulf me from all sides. I felt the treacherous
currents pulling me down, deeper into a sea of self-
pity and despair.

My doctor had just diagnosed a life-threatening
kidney disease silently at work within my body. I felt
lost, alone, cheated of fulfilling the beautiful dreams
my husband and I shared for our future.

Days and weeks passed in a blur. Haunting
thoughts of death and dying nibbled away at my
inner being. I sobbed out my hurt and anger to God.

*Lord, this isn't fair. I've served You with my whole
heart. Why are You allowing this to happen to me?*

*What have I done to deserve this?*

My mind raced on with unanswerable questions. How many years did my husband and I still have together? How would my husband cope without me? Would I live to see my grandchildren grow up?

Darkness brought hopelessness and despair. My tears flowed freely but silently into my pillow. I felt ashamed of my weakness. I wanted to be strong, but strength and courage eluded me.

As time passed, I realized I couldn't go on like this. Somewhere, buried beneath my anger, resentment, and fear, flickered a spark of faith in the God who loved me. I wanted to rekindle that faith.

Like a drowning person, I pleaded, *Jesus, please help me! I can't face this alone. Please take away the fear and hopelessness I'm feeling.*

Jesus was there, waiting patiently for me to take my eyes off myself and focus on Him. Gradually, day by day, I felt the heavy weight of despair begin to release its grip on my heart.

Darkness gave way to light. Once again I opened my eyes to the beauty of God's blessings in my life— a loving and understanding husband, Christian children, friends who cared about me. The list went on and on.

As I praised God for these blessings, I felt His compassionate love enveloping me like a warm feathery quilt on a chilled winter night. His arms reached down to me. His strong hands gripped mine and lifted me gently upward, freeing me at last from the receding ice waters.

I know the Lord will never leave me. Whatever the future holds, we will face it together. His abundant, everlasting love has dissolved discouragement, fear, and doubt and replaced them with hope, peace, and joy.

*Dear Lord, You are my strength and my joy. Help me to see each new day as a precious gift from You. Help me to share Your love and hope with others, that they, too, may experience Your comfort and peace. Amen.*

Analie Smith, besides writing, enjoys camping, hiking, nature watching, reading, and music. In addition, she is active in the women's ministry program in her church. Analie is married and has three grown children. The Smiths make their home in La Mirada, California.

# Learning to Let Go

**Lou Ann Smith**

*The Lord will keep you from all
harm—he will watch over your life;
the Lord will watch over your coming
and going both now and forevermore.*
Psalm 121:7-8, *NIV*

I didn't think I would ever stop
crying. Maybe this was all a terrible mistake. Had I
made the wrong decision?

At thirteen, my daughter Jacque wanted to travel
to Hungary and Russia for the entire summer with a
missionary team. Together we prayed for guidance
and confirmation. My prayers were pretty smug at
first. After all, God would never take such a young
girl away from her mother for over two months.
Would He? I was sure I knew His answer to our
petitions.

When Jacque was an infant, her daddy and I
ceremonially dedicated her to the Lord like many
parents do during a Sunday morning church service.
At four years old she stood with her Sunday School

class in front of our congregation. Like an angelic miniature choir they sang, "This little light of mine, I'm gonna' let it shine," with one finger pointed high in the air. "Dat was my pretend candle," Jacque told her daddy afterwards.

Nearly ten years later I watched as a blossoming young woman joined about 1,000 other teen missionaries who were being commissioned to take the Good News into forty foreign countries. Each one held high a lighted candle. "This little light of mine," they sang in harmony. No pretending. They meant to make a difference in a dark and needy world.

It's easy to dedicate a baby to the Lord, but watching that baby grow and fulfill long-ago promises can be heartrending. Even when the releasing is into God's hand, it's hard to let go of our children.

That's why I phoned Shirley halfway through the summer. Her son Jim had traveled with a team to India. Shirley seemed so strong, so confident.

Sobbing into the receiver I confessed that I was worried about Jacque. Even though God had confirmed over and over that she was to go, and even though I prayed daily for her safety and we exchanged letters regularly, fear and doubt still visited me. "Sometimes," I wept, "I walk into her bedroom and pick up a lonely looking stuffed bear, hugging it and wondering if the summer will ever end and if everything will be OK."

"Lou Ann, do me a favor right after we hang up," Shirley counseled me. "Open your Bible to Psalm 121 and promise me you'll believe it."

What a surprise! When I turned to that wonderful passage, I saw that portions of it were underlined and that I had made a notation beside the last two verses. I had totally forgotten about it until that moment. It read: *February 2, 1988. This is my assurance as Jacque readies to go to Hungary and Russia.*

That was months before she even left! And yet God had promised to watch over her life and her "coming and going both now and forevermore."

I stopped crying. God kept His promise. And I learned that letting go at the right time for the right reasons with much prayer has great returns.

*Lord, thank You for Your comforting promises. Keep teaching me to trust You with my most precious treasures. Amen.*

Lou Ann Smith has written numerous articles and three children's books. Her book on the changes in a woman's life is a forthcoming title from Evergreen. She enjoys aerobics, singing, traveling, mothering, homemaking, and speaking at retreats. She and her husband, Kirby, have a son and a daughter and make their home in Cameron Park, California.

# Climbing Over Obstacles

**Vicki Snyder**

*With your help I can advance against
a troop; with my God I can scale a
wall.* Psalm 18:29, *NIV*

I looked at the test on the desk in
front of me. *This is it*, I thought. *If I pass, I'll
graduate and be free to look for a summer job. If I
don't, I'll have to take a summer daytime class,
leaving me no opportunity to earn income my family
needs.* I picked up the pencil and started writing.

I passed the test. I graduated. I found a job. But
once I had overcome these obstacles, different ones
took their place.

For years, I looked forward to the time when
obstacles would pass. Once we get this car paid off,
I'd think, our finances will be in good shape. Once
my husband finishes college, our lives will be less
hectic.

I was wrong. When we paid for the car, more expenses came along. After my husband graduated, other responsibilities demanded his time.

Obstacles didn't go away; they just changed. How was I going to deal with them?

David was a person who knew what obstacles were. When he was a shepherd, he had to be on twenty-four-hour alert for wild animals eager to attack his flock. Although he played his harp to soothe Saul's troubled spirit, he later had to flee when Saul tried to kill him. After David succeeded Saul as king, his own son Absalom tried to turn the Israelites against him.

Yes, David knew about obstacles, but he didn't let them stop him. Instead, he overcame them.

I realize that I can't wait until I take every test, pay every debt, and find my family free of outside responsibilities before I try to accomplish my goals. If I do, I'll never accomplish anything. Like David, when I conquer one obstacle, another is waiting.

So I'm thankful that, with God's help, I can march forward and, when I reach the wall, climb over.

*Thank You, God, for my newfound realization and for giving me strength to face and then to climb over obstacles. Amen.*

Vicki Snyder is a published writer who enjoys reading, walking, watching football and basketball, playing softball, and watching sunrises and sunsets. She and her husband, Lee, make their home in Kearney, Nebraska.

# No Blue Mondays

**Pauline E. Spray**

*Every day will I bless thee; and I will
praise thy name for ever and ever.*
Psalm 145:2, *KJV*

How are you today?" a professional man asked.

"It's Monday," the office worker snapped. That, according to her, said it all.

Contrarily, Monday is my favorite day. In fact, I like Mondays better than Saturdays. Children certainly would find that strange to believe, but it's true.

I enjoy getting up on Monday morning. After turning my thoughts heavenward, talking to God and reading His Word, I relish my breakfast while listening to the early newscast.

Once we lived in a beautiful area teeming with motels and restaurants. Each Monday morning we beat the professional blues by eating out. Furthermore, breakfast is the least expensive meal served in restaurants.

My husband and I cherish the memories of those mornings. We'll never forget the delicious breakfasts—eggs and bacon, complete with luscious cherry jam on homemade toast—eaten in that unique restaurant overlooking the bay, while on the outside, majestic swans languished on the water. Summer or winter, the scenery was terrific. It was especially fascinating on winter mornings when we plowed through blinding snow to keep our rendevous.

Now we enjoy going to McDonald's, where many of our friends gather regularly, for Danish, coffee, and a free newspaper.

Monday offers a forward look. It is the beginning of a new challenge. Who knows what the week will bring forth or what blessings God has in store?

I also like the routine that weekdays bring. I feel better living on schedule, planning, and later accessing what I have accomplished.

I know Sunday is the first day of the week. Both my Bible and calendar verify that fact. But Monday follows so closely on the heels of the Lord's day that it still offers time for reflection and evaluation. Last week I made mistakes, wasted time, and failed to make the most of the opportunities God gave me. But beginning today I shall strive to do better, to use my days to advantage and profit, endeavoring to fill them more meaningfully. I shall meditate on God's Word, love Him better, pray more, and sing His praises.

Every day should be filled with thankfulness and hymns of adoration, and Monday is a good time to begin.

*Every day will I bless You, O Lord—from one Monday until the next. You are worthy of my praise. Amen.*

Pauline E. Spray is the author of ten books and numerous articles. She is a schoolteacher, pastor's wife, speaker, mother, and grandmother who enjoys garage sales and crossword puzzles. Pauline and her husband have two daughters and make their home in Lapeer, Michigan.

# Victims of Grace

**Sharon Sterrenburg**

*Be gracious to me, O God, according
to Thy lovingkindness; According to
the greatness of Thy compassion, blot
out my transgressions.*
Psalm 51:1, *NASB*

I still remember the frustration on
my daughter's face when she told me, "Mom, I really
have a hard time with King David. I don't think he
deserves the title, 'A man after God's own heart.'" I
knew what was bothering her. One of her Bible
professors at college was leaving his wife for another
woman, and since we were in the middle of her own
wedding plans, this hit too close to home.

And she was right. David's actions with
Bathsheba and her husband, Uriah, were deplorable.
He committed most of the "big ones": adultery, lying,
betrayal of a friend, murder, and attempted cover-up.
Yet this sinner dared ask God's forgiveness, and God
abundantly gave it. Why?

I began studying David's prayer of repentance in

Psalm 51. He attempts to make no deals, no excuses; he doesn't even offer to do penitence. The great king of Israel, the mightiest warrior of his time, the writer of breathtaking songs, had nothing to offer that could earn forgiveness. He came with only one plea, *According to Thy lovingkindness.*

Looking up the word *lovingkindness*, I found the root was based in a covenant word. When two people made a contract, each had their responsibilities. But *hesed* (the word translated "lovingkindness") added a dimension unheard of in legal circles. It literally means that one of the parties "goes far beyond what is required."

God is not hiding this fact about Himself. Try counting the number of times lovingkindness is used in the Bible. Forgiveness is ours because of the way He is, not the way we are. It is for His name's sake that He pardons our iniquities (Psalm 25:11).

David understood this, and that is why he is called a man after God's own heart. It is not because he had a heart like God's, but rather, he had a fix on God's heart. David understood lovingkindness.

The plain truth is, I am in the same boat as David. If I had to come to God because of who I am or what I have done, I literally would not have a prayer. But I can come because of His lovingkindness—His willingness to go far beyond what is required. I am shipwrecked on God's lovingkindness and stranded on His forgiveness. What a place to be!

*Dear Father, like David, I dare not come to You on any merits of my own. But I can come boldly into Your presence because of Your lovingkindness. Thank You for not only forgiving me, but for lavishing forgiveness on me. Amen.*

Sharon Sterrenburg is a published author and founder of Titus Touch Ministries. In addition, she is a retreat speaker and enjoys traveling, reading, and cooking. Sharon and her husband, Don, have two children and reside in La Mirada, California.

# Camping Alone at Age Seventy

**Betty C. Stevens**

*For in the time of trouble he shall
hide me in his pavilion: in the secret
of his tabernacle shall he hide me ... I
will sing, yea, I will sing praises unto
the Lord.* Psalm 27:5-6, *KJV*

Camping by myself at age
seventy was something I was looking forward to. I
had been with my family (daughter, son-in-law, and
grandson) on several trips and weekends, so I knew
about trailer camping. But this whole week by
myself would be a special time, perhaps like a
spiritual retreat.

The first night it rained constantly. I didn't mind;
the trailer was dry, and the pelting rain lulled me to
sleep. Then waking up to a clear, sunshiny morning,
I walked in boot-clad feet down camp trails and
examined meadow wildflowers—all delightful

experiences. I went to bed early, tired but refreshed from being outdoors in God's wonderful world.

About 2 A.M. on the second night, I was suddenly awakened with roaring thunder and flashing lightning. I reached for the light and found the power had gone off. I sat on the edge of my bunk and prayed. Then I put on my slippers and robe.

I wasn't terribly afraid, just a little so. I found my flashlight and my Bible and turned to a favorite Psalm, the twenty-seventh. So many parts of this Psalm are special to me. But that night verses 5 and 6 stood out like a beacon. I started to sing some hymns: "Simply Trusting," "Amazing Grace," "Jesus Is All the World to Me," and the chorus: "Bless the Lord, O my soul, and all that is within me, bless His holy name."

As I continued to sing, interspersing prayers and praise, the tightness inside me lessened, and before long I was able to calmly and trustingly wait for the storm to be over.

*Thank You, Jesus, for Your presence and Your protection around me that night. Thank You for that very special time with You. Amen.*

Betty C. Stevens has written several articles, devotions, newspaper feature stories, and children's stories. She serves as prayer coordinator for a childhood center and Christian academy, writing monthly prayer letters and newsletter articles. Betty has one grown daughter and lives in Pittsburgh, Pennsylvania.

# *God in a Box!*

**Rondi Tangvald**

*Trust in Him at all times, O people;*
*Pour out your heart before Him; God*
*is a refuge for us.* Psalm 62:8, *NASB*

I took down the worn box from the top shelf of my closet, blew off the dust, and untied the string. Inside, safe and protected, lay my great-grandmother's Bible.

While flipping through the pages of this family treasure, I thought: Sometimes this is how I treat God. I keep Him in a box. I only take Him down, blow off the dust, and use Him when I want something or need Him to help me.

Then, when I've finished using Him, I put Him back in the box, tie it up with string, and stick Him high on the shelf until I need Him again.

What kind of God does that make him? Only a God of CONVENIENCE!

You see, I have incorrectly been depending upon myself, making all my own decisions, trusting my own judgments—only calling upon God when I need

Him for something.

How selfish of me! I have everything backward. Instead, I need to make my God an ever-present companion; an everyday best friend; someone to talk to, to call upon, to worship and praise, and to thank anytime—all the time! God needs to be a part of my daily walk, included in all of my life.

It's OK to pack my great-grandmother's Bible away in a box and set it on the shelf, but my God doesn't belong on a shelf. He belongs with ME!

*Dear God, please be my constant companion. Be with me in times of joy as well as in times of need. And keep reminding me that I should never put You out of reach, in a box on the shelf, but that You belong near me every day—all the time! Amen.*

Rondi Tangvald is a high school junior who has co-authored two children's books. Besides writing, Rondi enjoys singing and being active in Young Life and her Lutheran Youth Group. She makes her home with her family in Spokane, Washington.

# A Wider Vision

**Faye Hill Thompson**

*Delight yourself in the Lord and he*
*will give you the desires of your heart.*
*Commit your way to the Lord; trust*
*in him and he will do this.*
Psalm 37:4-5, *NIV*

Roll down the car window, my
sister motioned to me as we backed out of her
driveway after a weekend visit. "There's something I
meant to ask you," she voiced. "Do you care if we
come to Florida the same week that you're there to
visit the folks?"

I began having an anxiety attack. Why couldn't
they wait and come the week after us? There would
be more bedroom space. Didn't she know I wanted to
be alone with Mom? Such selfish excuses raced
through my mind. How could I tell my sister what I
really thought? I couldn't.

The night before we left for Florida the Lord and
I had a talk. "If You like giving me the desires of my
heart, Lord, then why is it working out just the

opposite of how I wanted things to be? I'll trust You to show me Your answer."

When we arrived in Florida, I noticed my sister didn't greet us in her usual bouncy manner. "I'm going to have a baby, but it isn't going so well," she spoke softly.

Throughout the next day my sister's physical condition weakened. That night she clasped my hand. "I'm so thankful that you're here with me, Sis. I need your presence to get me through this. Think of all the nights we're apart; the night I need you most, we're together."

The following day my sister miscarried. Returning from the hospital she wept on my shoulder. "My baby's gone, but you're here to support me."

Alone later I reflected on the happenings of the past two days as the Lord and I again talked. "God, You granted to me what I would have desired had I been able to see the whole picture as You could. You knew that I would never have missed this precious time to be with my sister."

Sometimes it takes an experience like this to realize that God grants me my desires but not necessarily the way I envision them. His is the wider vision.

*Help me to commit and trust myself to Your wider vision, Lord. Amen.*

Faye Hill Thompson is a former junior and senior high school teacher who enjoys writing, reading, traveling, and attending cultural events. She is office manager for her family's farm corporation. The Thompsons have one daughter and make their home in Ellsworth, Iowa.

# Wrapped in Swaddling Clothes

**Doris Toppen**

*But as for me, the nearness of God is
my good; I have made the Lord God
my refuge, that I may tell of all Thy
works.* Psalm 73:28, *NASB*

I reached down to gather up our
miniature village Christmas scene and to put the
figures away for another season. The deer grazing
around the pond had tipped over onto the "ice"
mirror. I turned on the lights in the snow-covered
cottages one last time. The homemade pinecone trees
that the children made years ago had been spruced
up with tiny balls and glitter by the grandchildren.
The gingerbread house needed a new coat of frosting
and maybe some shutters for the next year. Our
wonderland was almost too beautiful to put away.

Mary and Joseph reigned over the scene from the
hillside as always. The wisemen and shepherds

mingled with the angels. As I began to wrap the figures, I realized baby Jesus was gone.

I searched through the "neighborhood," behind the lampposts and snowdrifts, among the creatures in the valley and woodlands. I checked the candy-cane pathways and the evergreen arches.

Then I smiled. For lo, I found the babe wrapped in swaddling clothes—and lying with the teddy bear in the little red wagon. One of the grandchildren must have decided the celebration was over and it was time to move the baby out of the manger.

I pondered at the wisdom of it all. I, too, must move Jesus out of the manger and into each moment of my life. The celebration is just beginning. Each day is God's gift to me wrapped in the glitter of fading stardust and tied in ribbons of crimson dawn. As I learn to give more and live more at Christmastime, I take that hope and praise down the pathway and into real, practical, everyday experiences.

That's where I live—on the hillsides and in the valleys, punctuated by highs and lows. By looking through God's window perhaps I can shed light to brighten my neighborhood. I can share the power of Jesus that changes stress, sorrow, and darkness into joy and a gathering of simple, daily miracles.

Christmas is just a memory now in my treasury file. But I keep that love and joy alive when I remember to move Jesus out of the manger and keep Him in my heart.

*Dear Lord, help me to share daily my Christmas morning joy. May I be found walking with You, leaping and praising, serving and listening, faithfully pulling my little red wagon. Amen.*

Doris Toppen is a published writer who enjoys gardening, biking, teaching aerobics, hiking, public speaking, swimming, and being active in her church and community. Doris and her husband, Harvey, have four children and make their home in North Bend, Washington.

# When I Awake

**Tina Torres**

*When I awake, I will be satisfied with
seeing your likeness.*
Psalm 17:15, *NIV*

**M**om, it's so nice to wake up and
see you there."

What music to my ears! My sixteen-year-old
daughter had just awakened after major surgery and
was coming out of the anesthesia. She was groggy
but glad to see me through the haze. After all our
parent/teenager differences, it was nice to know she
still needed me there at the hospital, at least for a
little while.

I realized this was a fleeting situation so was
determined to savor it for all it was worth. As I
thought about her words, I immediately said to
myself, "That sounds like the Lord!" He's always
there. And He always will be. There is never a time
that He is not available, or too busy, or away
somewhere. Whenever I look up, He is there. I may
want to be there for my daughter whenever she

needs me but have no assurance that I will be able to. None of us knows how long we have on this earth, but God is utterly dependable. What a tremendous comfort!

I turned to look at her again. I looked at her open, vulnerable expression and felt a deep desire to hold her close and protect and take care of her. And I understood more how my declaration of dependence on God will move Him to put His arms of love and protection around me. God is the ultimate Parent— strong and tender, just and merciful, full of power and compassion. And He loves to hear me say how much I love to see His face.

*Lord, thank You for being there every time I wake up or look up. It's just a little taste of what it will be like when I see You face to face! Amen.*

Tina Torres is a Spanish translator/interpreter who lived in Mexico City for thirteen years. She is currently employed by an engineering firm. Tina enjoys evangelism, being involved with her church's mission committee, and writing. She is the mother of two grown children and resides in San Mateo, California.

# *Oasis of Love*

### Peggy Trim

*God sets the lonely in families, he
leads forth the prisoners with singing;
but the rebellious live in a sun-
scorched land.* Psalm 68:6, *NIV*

I don't tell my daughter, *I love you*,
anymore.
She's nineteen, unmarried, and pregnant.

After high school graduation she moved to the
city where she strained for the independence
she already had.

Stubbornness turned to rebellion;
rebellion manifested itself in alcohol and drug
abuse and immorality.

My daughter doesn't say, *I love you*, anymore.
She says, *I'm pregnant.*

Conversations explode, subside, and explode
again.
Each punctuated with, *Why?*

*I don't know, Mom.*
*When I was home you were always busy.*
*I thought you didn't love me.*
*I thought the family didn't care about me.*
*I went to my room and waited.*
*I felt so lonely ... .*

*I thought you preferred being in your room*
*to being with me.*
*I kept busy, waiting for you,*
*hoping you would come to me.*
*I felt so lonely ... .*

Weeks pass.
No angry arguments.
No controlled words.
No tearful embraces.
No letters, no phone calls.

Weeks of looking within.
*What needs to change in me?*

Weeks of looking up.
Learning the sacrifice of thanksgiving.
Learning that verbs like wait and hope and trust
are active, though profoundly still.

Weeks of looking outward to friends—
friends who are friends of God.
Through prayer they direct His compassion
   toward us.

Then my daughter remembers the God of her
   childhood
and she is reconciled to Him—

releasing us from our prisons of loneliness.
Everyday we experience His power
to mend our broken relationship.

But, we still don't say, *I love you*.
Now we say, *I know that you love me*.

*Lord, continue to guide the rebellious to repentance
and to the oasis of Your love. Amen.*

Peggy Trim is a mother of five and grandmother of four who
is working on her college degree. Besides writing she enjoys
reading and knitting. Peggy and her husband have nurtured
twelve foster children besides their own family. They reside
in Methow, Washington.

# A View at 37,000 Feet

**Ann Udell**

*When I am afraid, I will trust in you.*
Psalm 56:3, *NIV*

Flight 306 is now boarding at gate 14," announced a pleasant voice over the loudspeaker.

Not wanting to stand out as a novice flyer, I attempted to adopt the composure and attitude of the apparently seasoned travelers around me. This prevented the little girl inside me from shouting, "Hey, everybody, this is my first ride on a 747 jet and my first visit to New York City. I am so excited! I am also very frightened."

I walked through the tunnel, boarded the plane, and located my seat by a window. Recalling a verse from the Psalms, I uttered a prayer and folded my quivering hands to prevent clutching the arm of the person beside me. As the plane took off, we headed west, over the Pacific Ocean. Then banking, we turned east and climbed higher and higher. Shortly the pilot announced we were at 37,000 feet.

Only the differing ground patterns indicated we were moving, since the flight was so smooth. Then the earth below was no longer visible due to a thick cover of clouds. A brilliant yellow sun and clear blue sky bordered the clouds above so they appeared as blankets of freshly picked cotton, and below, a sea of billowy white stretched as far as I could see. I felt suspended in time and space.

*How similar the clouds are to life,* I thought. They appear to be filled with great substance, so that if you fell they would catch you and cushion your fall. Yet that perception of beauty and softness is deceptive. They block the sun, which we depend on for light and a sense of direction, and their density can cause us to lose our way.

Soon we would be landing. An inner peace had replaced my anxiety. As thankful as I was for the pilot's special instruments to direct him in poor visibility, I was filled with a greater awe for the instrument of God's Word. Through it, He guides and directs me in times of darkness and doubt and assures me of His constant presence.

*Father God, thank You for the gift of Your Word and its presence and power in my life. Amen.*

Ann Udell is a writer, as well as a speaker for retreats and women's meetings. She serves as president of her church's women's ministry and enjoys traveling, camping, cooking, gardening, and interior decorating. Ann and her husband have three grown children and make their home in Atascadero, California.

# Your Praise and Your Glory All the Day!

**Chris Ulmer**

*I have become a wonder to many, but
You are my strong refuge. Let my
mouth be filled with Your praise and
with Your glory all the day.*
Psalm 71:7-8, *NKJV*

**M**y grandmother Nettie
Bloomgren lived a full life! Born in the 1800s, as a
young girl she had dated in a horse and buggy; she
saw the first car ever to drive into town; spoke on
the first telephone around; and, yes, lived to see, via
television, Neil Armstrong take man's first step on
the moon.

And then, "Brain cancer, two weeks to live," the
doctor told her. Her family all agreed that she had

lived a good life and was ready to meet her Lord.

Grandmother went to a rest home to spend the last two weeks of her life. There were good days and there were bad days, but through it all, she was still able to praise her God. Two weeks went by, and then two months, and she lived on.

During this time, she learned that I was pregnant with her first great-grandchild; she also knew that God wasn't ready to take her home. She began to improve, and her brain and body were restored. She lived for sixteen more years, praying for and leading many to the Lord right there in the rest home.

She truly was "a wonder to many," for God was her strong refuge. And her mouth was filled with His praise and glory "all the day"—until her last.

*Father God, thank You for a grandmother who taught me by example of Your love and grace. I ask, dear Father, that You use me, too, as I sing Your praises. Amen.*

Chris Ulmer codirects, with her husband, Ray, His Kids Music Ministries. She enjoys sailing and sewing. The Ulmers have two sons and one daughter and make their home in Ventura, California.

# Never on
# A Shelf

**Marcia Van't Land**

*They will still bear fruit in old age,*
*they will stay fresh and green.*
Psalm 92:14, *NIV*

Lately, it has become necessary to
call a substitute to take my place as a Bible study
leader. Because of a lingering disability, this
situation has happened repeatedly over the past
eleven years.

One day a woman approached me and asked,
"How does it feel to be put on a shelf?" I was so
shocked by her question, I almost fell out of my
wheelchair. Do people think of me as being *on a
shelf*? Because of my disability, am I no longer able
to do Christian service?

In our society, we have mandatory retirement,
nursing homes for the elderly, legal abortions of
suspected retarded or handicapped babies, and,
sometimes with little regard, we pull the plug on
comatose patients. We are inundated with the idea
that the elderly and those mentally or physically

handicapped are useless in our society.

As I think about the Old Testament, I am reminded that no one retired. Kings were kings until they died. Prophets never went out of office. And as far as disabilities, Moses had a speech impediment and the apostle Paul had a "thorn in his side" that God chose not to heal.

I read an article recently by a woman who cared for her elderly mother who was in the final stages of Parkinson's disease, causing her to often forgot her family and surroundings. One day the mother seemed to be making moaning sounds in her sleep. When her daughter asked what was wrong, the mother managed to communicate that she was not moaning, she was praying. The daughter then joined her in prayer.

God always has a purpose for our lives. He never retires us from the Christian life. In God's eyes we are never put on a shelf.

*Thank You, God, that You can use us, no matter what our age or physical or mental ability. Help me to continually see my purpose in life so I can glorify You in all that I do. Amen.*

Marcia Van't Land has written numerous articles for a variety of magazines and the book *Ya Gotta Have Hope* (Evergreen, 1992). A former schoolteacher, she makes her home in Chino, California, with her husband, Tom, and three children.

# Wait, God!

**Kara Vaughan**

*O Lord, open my lips, and my mouth*
*will declare your praise.*
Psalm 51:15, *NIV*

I walked into her room and sat down across from her on the floor; we giggled about old times.

Inside, my heart was pounding as I searched for the words to share my heart with her, my best friend for over eight years. *If Christ is number one in my life*, I thought, *then someone as special to me as Lisa needs to know it.* Before going to Lisa's house, I had prayed with some friends that I would be able to communicate effectively what Christ had done for her and that she would hear my message.

Lisa and I had discussed the meaning of Christianity before in one of our many talks about the meaning of life, but I had never presented it to her on the personal basis that I wanted to that night. Sharing the gospel has always scared me, and sharing Jesus with Lisa scared me more than anything, mainly because I was afraid she would reject what I had to say, and reject me! I began to think of all the reasons why "tonight isn't such a good night." Couldn't God be a little more patient?

Suddenly, before I could even get the words out, Lisa asked me to share what it means to live your life for Christ! Emotions welled up inside me as I shared with her how long I had been waiting for this opportunity, and then I began to give her a glimpse of the Christ I know.

God had been patient with me all along. And when the time was right, He had given me the right words to speak. How often I forget what He can do if only I trust in His timing and rely on Him to be the strength of my life!

*Lord, thank You for Your patience, Your perfect timing, and for being my strength! Amen.*

Kara Vaughan is a Westmont College student who loves the ocean and who enjoys writing poetry, working with teens, singing, and playing volleyball. She makes her home with her family in Ventura, California.

# *Precious in His Sight*

**Cynthia Ann Wachner**

*O Israel, hope in the Lord! For with
the Lord there is steadfast love, and
with him is plenteous redemption.
And he will redeem Israel from all
his iniquities.* Psalm 130:7-8, *RSV*

While at the junk store I found
an old goblet caked with gritty soil. A few bare spots
looked like gunky old plastic I'd seen in the gutter.
As I picked it up, the grit scratched my fingers and
the weight of the mud inside surprised me. I almost
left the goblet there. But, thinking it might have
great value, I purchased it for the necessary price.

At home I rubbed it with cleansing cream and
discovered a delicately etched crystal goblet. As I
held it up to the sunbeams shining through my
kitchen window, it glistened like a rainbow of light. I
filled it with sparkling cool water and sipped. As the
water slid past my lips, it refreshed me in the
summer's heat. Joy flooded my soul and I rejoiced as
I realized I had something rare and of great value.

The goblet reminds me of God's love. Even while I am coated and filled with sin, He still sees value in me. He purchased me with the necessary price of Christ's sacrifice. Using Christ's blood He cleanses me so I radiate His love light. Then, He fills me with the living water of His righteousness and goodness. My actions shine with His love and I impart His refreshment to thirsty souls around me. He keeps me without spot. I am His priceless possession.

*Father, hold me and cleanse me from all sin. Fill me with Christ's goodness and righteousness. Let me experience Your love, share it with others, and know I am precious in Your sight. Amen.*

Cynthia Ann Wachner has written numerous articles, devotions, poems, and personality profiles. In addition, she represents other writers through her agency Good News Literary Service. She is the mother of a son and a daughter and resides in Visalia, California.

# A "Woolly" Lesson

**Shirley Pope Waite**

*The Lord is my shepherd; I shall not want.* Psalm 23:1, *KJV*

There's a dog wandering around on the highway! I hope it doesn't get hit!" I exclaimed. A drama unfolded outside our restaurant window that cold winter afternoon in Ellensburg, Washington.

We watched as a state patrolman left his vehicle. But it wasn't a dog he was after; it was a sheep, which apparently had jumped from a horse trailer when the owner had stopped to check on his several woolly passengers. Just then, the animal ran down an embankment.

Customers stopped eating; waitresses lingered in the dining area; all gawked out the large picture window. We watched the attempted rescue, until the frightened sheep disappeared behind a hillock.

As I turned back to my sandwich, I thought, *I'm like that sheep!* God wants to rescue me from the dangerous highways and steep embankments of life.

Too often I view Him as an officer of the law, yet in my heart I know that He is a God of love and mercy, the "Owner" who values me as His own precious child.

We finished our meal and left the restaurant before the final act of the drama. I've since wondered if that sheep now grazes contentedly with the rest of the flock, or if it got lost in the foothills surrounding Ellensburg.

I don't need to wonder about my future. Peace and contentment are mine when I surrender to the secure arms of my Owner, knowing His way is best. Jesus makes that very clear when He says: "I am the good shepherd; I know my sheep and my sheep know me" (John 10:14).

*Dear Lord, thank You for laying down Your life for me, one of Your sheep. Help me not to stray from Your loving arms. Amen.*

Shirley Pope Waite has written numerous articles, poems, and devotions. She teaches "Writing to Sell" and "Writing Your Memoirs" classes at community colleges in her area. Shirley enjoys reading, Bible study, working crossword puzzles, and traveling. She and her husband have six children and reside in Walla Walla, Washington.

# "OK, Mommy"

**Laurie Skye Wardwell**

*I desire to do your will, O my God;*
*your law is within my heart.*
Psalm 40:8, *NIV*

The girls were playing quietly in the family room when I sat down to take a well-deserved break. I had just put my head back and closed my eyes when a little hand touched my arm. There stood my three-year-old, excitement sparkling in her eyes.

"Mommy, can I do what I'm doin'?"

Puzzled by her question I asked, "What are you doin'?"

She did a dance of merriment, eyes jumping with her joy. "I'm doin' what I'm doin'! Can I do what I'm doin'"?

By now I was beginning to get suspicious. "Meghan, do you think you should be doin' what you're doin'?"

"No," she replied with a mischievous smile. "Can I do what I'm doin'?"

"Meghan, if you don't think you should be doing

what you're doing, then I think it's a good idea if you don't do it."

"OK, Mommy!" she said brightly as she skipped back to play with her sister.

I smiled and shook my head in wonder. I had no idea what she had been doing, just that she knew it was wrong. I felt as if I had been through a test and passed with high marks.

I chuckled as I thought of all the times I had tried to teach her right from wrong. This was a step toward independence; my little girl was growing up. Meghan's desire to please me was greater than her desire to do whatever it was she had been doing. It illustrated what the Psalmist said, "Your law is within my heart." She knew in her heart our law or rules.

We can have God's law in our hearts: to show us right from wrong; to help us know what to do or not do. As we read and study, dwell on and memorize, God's Word becomes established in our hearts.

Just as a parent teaches a child, the Lord teaches us to do His will. Psalm 143:10 says, "Teach me to do your will, for you are my God." The more we understand God's love for us, the more we desire to do His will. And we, like little children, want to please our heavenly Father.

*Lord, I desire to do Your will. Help me and guide me, by placing Your law in my heart. I want to please You. Amen.*

Laurie Skye Wardwell is the executive director of LOVE INC (Love in the Name of Christ) in her hometown. She enjoys reading, snowmobiling, and spending time with her family and friends. Laurie and her husband, Lance, have two children and reside in Reedley, California.

# Be in His Word!

**Candace Webb**

*Teach me Thy statutes.*
Psalm 119:26, *NASB*

For many years I have suffered from a compulsive eating disorder. About five years ago, the effects of this disorder were manifested in the form of an esophageal dysfunction that brought debilitating symptoms. My body responded poorly to all available medical treatments. I became fearful.

In desperation I phoned a local Christian church. Soon a woman from the church visited me. When she heard of my trials and tribulations, she counseled, "You need to be reading the Word of God." Now, I had been a believer since childhood but had not been rooted in His Word. In fact, I remember once saying that I didn't think a Christian needed to read the Bible.

This woman gave me her edition of *The Living Bible*. And from that day forward I have continued to be in God's Word.

Up until then God had refined me through the

process of life experiences, or should I say disasters? Disasters of choice as well as oppression.

Now the Lord is able to refine me through the knowledge of His ways versus the ways of the world. Through the reading of His Word, I receive peace, strength, healing, and comfort for all my fears.

I've learned that unless I'm "in" His Word and His Word is "in" me, I will not be submitting myself truly to the refining power, comfort, and healing ways of our Lord.

*Father, help me to hear Your voice through Your Word and through the gift of the Holy Spirit within me, as You guide me into Your ways. Enable me to trust all of my life to You. Amen.*

Candace Webb, in addition to writing, enjoys studying God's Word, ministering for the Lord, gardening, and landscaping. She is currently missions coordinator at her church and working on her Bachelor of Theology degree. She and her husband, Steven, have one son and make their home in Oxnard, California.

# Raspberries
# *for*
# Remembering

**Mildred Wenger**

*He brought me up also out of an
horrible pit, out of the miry clay, and
set my feet upon a rock, and
established my goings.*
Psalm 40:2, *KJV*

My daughter Barbara, who lives
two hundred miles away, was visiting last summer.
Since the raspberries were beginning to ripen, I
suggested we go out to the garden and see if we
could fill a few boxes for her to take home.

The berries were big and beautiful, sweet and
juicy; they were the nicest raspberries she had ever
seen. I asked her if she remembered where those
bushes had come from. She said she didn't.

I told her how her father had gone along the
stony fence rows and pulled the thin scraggy bushes
out from the rocks. He had transplanted them into
the rich garden soil and had weeded and watered
and mulched and pruned them, year after year. They
had responded to his loving care by growing into
these thick healthy plants, which produced lavish
crops of luscious berries.

I told her these bushes remind me of how God works. He takes a person who is poor and needy. He lifts him up and nurtures and helps him and makes him into a person whose life is fine and worthwhile.

"That's beautiful, Mom," she said. "You ought to write it down."

Psalm 40 says, "He brought me up also out of an horrible pit." We were all in the horrible pit of sin. Yet the Lord accepts us with our faults and failures and unlovely ways. He forgives us and transplants us into His family. Then He continually provides us with nourishment and guidance through His written Word and through the Holy Spirit. At times He prunes us by allowing circumstances that are difficult to understand. Yet He gives us courage to face whatever trials come. Our lives are made beautiful and productive because of the loving care our Lord lavishes upon us.

The raspberries are a constant reminder to me. Whenever I get a box out of the freezer to make a pie or some other dessert, I think back to that conversation in the garden. And I am grateful again for the wonderful ways God has worked in my life.

*Lord, let me never forget from where you have brought me and for saving me from what I might have become. I owe everything I have and am to You. Thank You, Jesus. Amen.*

Mildred Wenger has written numerous stories and articles and has edited church bulletins for over twenty years. She enjoys reading, music, and playing the keyboard for a local gospel quartet. Mildred and her husband, Daniel, have five grown children and reside in Stevens, Pennsylvania.

# Never Enough Time

**Marcy Weydemuller**

*The Lord will accomplish what concerns me.* Psalm 138:8, *NASB*

Today our youngest child is ill with the flu, and the minutes are creeping by while I wait for the fever and aches to subside. I want time to speed up.

Not like yesterday, a typical day of frustration, as I raced around playing beat the clock all day, and the clock won. I so often feel like Alice's rabbit running here and there, "I'm late, I'm late." Words like *later, not enough time,* or *not now* echo in my mind, and I fear my children will remember their mother as "too busy."

Unplanned days tend to be eaten up with trivialities, and the time set aside for quiet thinking slips away. Structured days don't fare much better. Depending on interruptions, I may or may not finish appointed tasks. Even if the day has ended with a to-do list fully crossed out, can I consider that the day has been an accomplishment if it's been done at the expense of listening, sharing, or tickling? Or perhaps, the day is one of caring and sharing but with only a few chores done. By what standard is the day a success or a failure?

I wonder, *Where is the balance, Lord? Is time friend or foe? Time seems such a precious gift, not to be wasted. That's the Martha in me, isn't it? Am I measuring my days in accomplishments instead of accepting each day as it comes from Your hand?*

I forget that God's work is also done in silence and in rest, so I let frustration chafe at me on quiet days. It's time for me to stop putting my to-do list out just expecting His stamp of approval instead of prayerfully listening to His directives. Then, just maybe, I can tolerate the hectic days and accept the unending ones knowing each has a purpose.

*Thank You, Lord, that You know before I do what needs to be accomplished and You lead me accordingly. Amen.*

Marcy Weydemuller has written book reviews, devotions, and short stories. A full-time homemaker, she enjoys cross-stitch and reading. She and her husband, Bob, have three children and reside in Concord, California.

# Suggestion Boxing

**Geraldine Wieland**

*I will praise the Lord, who counsels
me; even at night my heart instructs
me.* Psalm 16:7, *NIV*

When my husband and I read an
article which claimed that communication was the
most important of the marital arts, we thought some
psychologist had wiretapped our pet-peeve swap
meets. (This is where one spouse tries to sell the
other on the need for changing an irritating habit,
and the other doesn't buy the idea.)

Suddenly these lighthearted encounters took on
the tone of a summit meeting. The first item on the
agenda was my mate's disapproval of my holding the
refrigerator door open any longer than it took to grab
what I was after. No star-gazing allowed. No
lollygagging over leftovers. He wanted an open and
shut case. He also recommended that with a little
foresight I could have a group of perishables handy
for replacement.

My plan to open the refrigerator only when no

one was around worked well until we took a winter camping vacation, complete with icebox. Apparently, the fact that it was colder outside of the box than in it didn't excuse my lack of organization. Well, the block of ice may have been melting, but a frown was frozen on my face.

My words came straight from the North Pole as I accused, "Recreation should not be spoiled by unresolved gripes."

I slammed the icebox door and waited for an apology—which didn't come. That night I entreated the Lord to "speak to" my partner.

Instead, He began to thaw *my* stubbornness. Jesus spoke to me about my ungracious attitude toward most hints, no matter how helpful. Whereas my husband usually received correction with good humor, I'd been clinging to the glacier of arrogance. So, no more waiting for my opponent to relent. The offer of a cuddly reconciliation must come from me.

*Lord, soften my heart and give me a teachable spirit so that I may benefit from Your counsel. Amen.*

Geraldine Wieland writes articles, devotions, and poetry and edits her writers' group newsletter. Geraldine has worked many years with Child Evangelism Fellowship and has taught Bible classes for both women and children. The mother of six grown children, she resides in North Highland, California.

# A New Song, A New Day

**Lorraine Hope Wilkinson**

*He put a new song in my mouth, a
hymn of praise to our God.*
Psalm 40:3, *NIV*

What a chorus of birds we heard
this morning!

Most mornings my husband and I begin our day
with a fast walk around a long block, getting up and
out before much of our community is stirring. Now in
the spring, it is just dawn, before the sun begins its
circuit, before the insects begin their daily buzzing.
But not before the birds!

As we left our home this morning, we heard an
occasional chirp or peep from a tree here and there.
But as we rounded a corner, we realized that we
were entering an area filled with bird songs. Then
we were surrounded with an outpouring of song!
There were chirps from the sparrows (the percussion,
perhaps), the plaintive cooing of the mourning doves
(a mellow accompaniment), and the limitless variety
of solos from the mockingbirds. Each bird seemed to
be singing from his heart, singing a new song to the
new day, a song of praise for the Maker of the day.

Each day is a new day for me too. How will I
start the day? Sometimes I am reluctant to get up in
the morning and "this day that the Lord has made"

is off to a slow start right from the beginning. I wonder if the birds ever feel that way? I picture that when they wake up, they sense the presence of God in the dawn and are ready for a song of praise. Later they go find breakfast, knowing that God will supply that too.

Most of us know where breakfast is coming from, along with the provisions for the day. How natural and easy it would be for us to slip from our beds to our knees and there offer a simple prayer of praise and thanksgiving for the morning and of commitment of our day to the Lord.

And it is more than that! God wants to put a new song in my mouth! Just as that mockingbird has a never ending supply of songs, so the Lord has new things for me to do, an endless variety just for me, that will give me great joy and bring Him glory. In my home it could be rearranging the living room or making a fancy dessert. It could be a project shared with my child or a phone call or visit. Or a poem or devotion written from the heart. Maybe it is a change of attitude that allows the Lord to put a spring in my step and a song on my lips.

What is the new thing He has for me today? In my reluctance or boredom, will I miss it?

*Dear Lord, I want You to put Your new song in me today, so that my life will bring You praise and glory. I open myself to the possibilities of what this may be. Amen.*

Lorraine Hope Wilkinson is an author and partner of Legacy House publishing coordinators. Besides writing she enjoys sewing, knitting, playing piano and organ, reading, editing, and teaching Bible studies. She and her husband have six children and make their home in West Hills, California.

# Uphill Climb

**Esther Wilkison**

*Cast thy burden upon the Lord, and
he shall sustain thee: he shall never
suffer the righteous to be moved.*
Psalm 55:22, *KJV*

It was the culmination of our two
weeks of staff training before we launched into a
summer as camp counselors. It was a tradition to
take a late night hike up Soldier Mountain, have a
big bonfire by the wooden cross, and then sleep on a
sand dune near the top. The director thought it an
excellent way to "sand off" the city-slicker side of our
nature and toughen us up for the rigors of camp
work.

About 9:00 P.M., we headed out with bedrolls and
canteens. I'm not the wilderness type, but I was
determined to stay right behind the leader, a six-foot-
five mountain man. Everyone kept a fast pace as we
headed down the dry river bed, but as the trail
steepened, the ranks near the leader thinned. He
must have been amused by my attempt to keep up.
My hard breathing betrayed my true physical
condition. As the path got steeper and the wind blew

stronger, he asked if he could carry my bedroll.

"Oh, no," I replied. "I'm doing fine." He shrugged, and we continued.

As the moon traveled across the sky, it seemed we had been hiking for hours but still the peak was far ahead. The path was extremely steep and sandy, making it hard to get a good hold and make progress. The wind whipped furiously and I could hardly keep up. Again the leader asked if he could carry my bedroll. Meekly, I slid it off my shoulders and handed it to him, feeling like I was admitting defeat. When we started up again, however, it was so much easier to keep up, and we could go much faster. I wondered why I hadn't given him my pack the first time he asked. After all, he was much more capable than I.

*Father, this load of care, the problems that are weighing me down, You asked for them before. I'm willing to humble myself and give them to You now. Amen.*

Esther Wilkison is a school teacher, sponsor, and coach for volleyball, basketball, and cheerleading. Besides writing she enjoys biking, hiking, and swimming. Esther makes her home in Phoenix, Arizona.

# *Watered by the Spirit, Warmed by the Son*

**Betty Willems**

*I will meditate on the glorious splendor of Your majesty, And on Your wondrous works.*
Psalm 145:5, *NKJV*

A single yellow daffodil on the table ministered silently to me, as a friend and I carried on our idle chatter over lunch. Neither of us mentioned that lone daffodil standing regally in its crystal vase, yet it spoke volumes to my heart.

After weeks of winds and rain, it painted for me a glorious living picture of the delightful spring day that God had given. Spring was here at last—all eighty-four degrees of it! My heart rejoiced. Winter had not lasted forever. The daffodil's yellow throat seemed to proclaim a miracle, the miracle of hope out of despair, of life out of death.

It brought to mind a summer day when my spade had turned up a bulb in my garden, its leaves withered and brown. The bulb was drained and lifeless looking. I left it buried in its resting place. Yet, the following spring when it had been watered by the rain and warmed by the sun, life and beauty sprang forth—a true symbol of the resurrection. From what seemed dead, life had burst forth.

I especially needed that reminder today. It was my mother's birthday. She had enjoyed almost ninety of them. Now she was with the Lord. Mothers are people you never forget. I miss her still. It was comforting to know that because she had been watered by the Spirit and warmed by the Son, she, too, has burst the bonds of death that seemed to hold her captive. I can have hope instead of despair, because I live on the victorious side of Easter.

I didn't reveal these thoughts to my friend as we sipped our coffee. The timing wasn't right. But I learned that day to be aware of how the Holy Spirit can speak through the everyday, commonplace things in life. He can speak anywhere. His voice is always there, but our ears are not always tuned to it. The message of the daffodil was precious to me. I'm glad I didn't pass it by with only a casual glance.

*Dear Lord, teach me to be sensitive to Your Spirit. Give me ears to hear Your voice and eyes that are focused on the spiritual dimension. Amen.*

Betty Willems is a free-lance writer, having published several magazine articles and book reviews. Betty and her husband, Jim, have four grown children and make their home in Post Falls, Idaho.

# A Sentry Guards My Lips

**Nancy Witmer**

*Set a guard over my mouth, O Lord;*
*keep watch over the door of my lips.*
Psalm 141:3, *NIV*

Hi, Judy. Did you hear the latest about Roger and Marilyn?" I dropped a box of cereal into my shopping cart and steered it to the side of the aisle.

"Now what?" Judy asked.

"Marilyn got a curly perm and Roger hates it. He told her that either she could wear a hat until the perm grows out or she could go live with her mother."

"That sounds like Roger," Judy said. "He's so unreasonable. I don't know why Marilyn puts up with him."

"Well, he is loaded and some people will do anything for money," I said, knowingly. I glanced at my watch. "I must get moving. I have to teach Sunday School tomorrow, and I haven't even looked at the lesson yet."

"Bye. See you in church. I wonder if Roger and Marilyn will be there."

"Oh, they wouldn't miss church," I said. "It's part

of their image. But I can't wait to see if Marilyn will be wearing a hat." I laughed and pushed my cart toward the front of the supermarket.

Later, as I tried to prepare my Sunday School lesson, my mind flashed back to that conversation with Judy. A still, small voice inside me struggled to be heard. I tried to ignore it, but it refused to be silenced. "You were gossiping again," it said. "Gossip is a sin, too, you know."

My conscience and I had been through similar dialogues before. I knew all the Scriptures about how seemingly innocent words can kindle fires, spread discord, and ruin relationships. I knew what the Bible had to say about words; my problem was applying those principles to the words I spoke.

"Forgive me, Lord," I prayed. "I can't do this alone. I need your help to overcome the sin of gossip."

In the days and years since that prayer, God has helped me by placing the Holy Spirit on guard-duty at the door of my mouth. When I am tempted to repeat unkind or unflattering news about someone, this heavenly sentry reminds me that I am about to gossip. When I ignore His warning, He convicts me of my sin and calls me to repentance.

*Lord, I need Your help to keep my words uplifting and wholesome. I invite Your Spirit to guard my lips today. Amen.*

Nancy Witmer is a free-lance writer and has published numerous articles and devotions. Nancy enjoys reading, traveling, and camping with her family. In addition, she is a board member of St. David's Christian Writers' Conference. The Witmers have two grown sons and reside in Manheim, Pennsylvania.

# Grandma Still Speaks

**Kitty Snead Yarchin**

*You must never worship any other
god, nor ever have an idol in your
home.* Psalm 81:9, *TLB*

Excitement rose as my husband
and I talked about our priceless treasure. We had
tied the cherished heirloom to the top of the car and
were taking it home with us after visiting my
parents. It was my grandmother's spinning wheel.

As we covered the miles, I relived the long love
affair I had had with this precious antique. When I
was only a little girl, I had sat at Grandma Snead's
feet and watched her card wool and spin it into yarn.
The hum and click-click of the wheel came to be a
soothing sound as Grandma told me stories of her
early life. She quoted Scriptures and sang songs
until I knew them by heart.

The spinning wheel, linked so closely to my
memories of her, was now my very own. I could
hardly wait to show it off.

We stopped again and again to check the ropes

that held it in place. At home my husband propped the fragile wheel and its parts against the garage wall. "I'll assemble this on Saturday," he said.

All week I arranged and rearranged furniture to find the right place for the spinning wheel. It merited a proper place of honor.

As I returned home from shopping on Friday, my mind was filled with dinner plans. Preoccupied, I drove into our open garage, and ... crunch.

*Oh, no! The spinning wheel*, I thought as I leaped from the car. The wheel had fallen over on the floor and I hadn't seen it. Now I'd smashed it to smithereens. Uncontrollable sobs welled up. Grief-stricken, I bent over the hood of the car and let the tears flow.

Presently a lesson that Grandma had taught me brought to mind an old hymn: "The dearest idol I have known, whate'er that idol be; help me to tear it from thy throne, and worship only thee."

Years have passed since that traumatic experience, yet Grandma's words still chide me when I become overly attached to things.

I lost a spinning wheel, but I gained a new perspective.

*Dear Father, help me never to cherish anything so much that it becomes an idol. May I always worship only You. Amen.*

Kitty Snead Yarchin is a published writer who enjoys reading, interior decorating, entertaining, and, with her husband, leading a church home group. In addition, she is a member of the San Diego County Christian Writers' Guild. The Yarchins have four children and make their home in Carlsbad, California.

# It's Not My Fault!

**Paula Meiners Yingst**

*Then I acknowledged my sin to you
and did not cover up my iniquity. I
said, "I will confess my transgressions
to the Lord"—and you forgave the
guilt of my sin.* Psalm 32:5, *NIV*

The Sunday School lesson theme
was praying for forgiveness, and I asked my eager
second graders, "Have any of you done something
wrong this week that you'd like to share with the
class?" The gregarious group fell silent, each child
peering guiltily at another as though they'd just been
accused of some unpardonable offense.

I was beginning to consider rephrasing my
question when Faith, an auburn-haired cherub with
a sprinkling of freckles across her pert nose,
solemnly commented, "Well, I didn't do anything
wrong, but my brother did!"

Immediately, the tense atmosphere dissipated
and streams of uninhibited gossip began flowing
from the mouths of the other children. Their relieved
expressions were comical. How much easier it was
for them to recognize and point out someone else's
faults!

I sympathized with the children's anxious

reactions. No one enjoys being singled out when sin is the topic of discussion. I sometimes wonder how the Samaritan woman felt when she realized Jesus was miraculously aware of her shameful reputation. Was Martha offended when her Lord admonished her fretful behavior? What emotions raged within Peter after Jesus predicted his unfaithfulness? Did Judas' heart thump wildly within his breast as he uttered the words, "Surely not I, Rabbi?"

All too often, it seems, we find ourselves pointing an accusing finger at a struggling brother or sister in Christ while failing to recognize our own, equally sinful shortcomings.

David recognized his sinful tendencies and experienced the cleansing power of confession and forgiveness. He wrote, "When I kept silent, my bones wasted away ... my strength was sapped as in the heat of summer. Then I acknowledged my sin to you ... and you forgave the guilt of my sin" (Psalm 32:3-5).

David also realized the benefit of accepting God's gift of grace: "Blessed is the man whose sin the Lord does not count against him and in whose spirit is no deceit" (Psalm 32:2).

*Heavenly Father, thank You for granting me forgiveness when I'm humble enough to ask for it. And help me remember to reach out with compassion instead of pointing my finger. Amen.*

Paula Yingst is a creative writing and communication consultant with the Vista Unified School District. She is a free-lance writer and has had several magazine articles published. Paula and her husband, Chuck, have one daughter and one son and make their home in Vista, California.

# God's Apricot Tree

**Grazia Patt Yonan**

*Blessed is the man who does not walk
in the counsel of the wicked or stand
in the way of sinners or sit in the seat
of mockers. But his delight is in the
law of the Lord, and on his law he
meditates day and night. He is like a
tree planted by streams of water,
which yields its fruit in season and
whose leaf does not wither. Whatever
he does prospers.* Psalm 1:1-4, *NIV*

A flourishing apricot tree lives on
the grounds of an old Victorian estate next door to
our former home. The stately mansion has been
abandoned for several years, yet each year the city
sends in a crew to clear weeds. Though the English
walnut tree on that property has tiny walnuts due to
lack of irrigation, the apricot tree gives forth a
bountiful harvest each alternate year, as most
healthy apricot trees do. The tree has become the
delight of neighborhood children, who cut through

the property on their way to a nearby playground.

*How does this tree do it,* I wondered, *when all the other trees seem so neglected?*

"This tree is watered by an underground stream," a gardener friend explained. "The soil is excellent and the occasional rainfall helps, but it is the stream that really makes a difference!"

God's apricot tree soon became a daily reminder to me of His faithfulness and grace. Like the tree, I need the daily nourishment of the rich, fertile ground of God's Word, in which I need to be rooted. I, too, am sustained by underground streams of His Holy Spirit, even as I am showered and refreshed by the rain of His love and daily provision. Like the apricot tree, I can look forward to the spiritual prosperity God promises, as I bring forth fruit at His appointed time!

*Dear heavenly Father, thank You for Your faithfulness. How exciting it is to know that as I delight in Your Word, You refresh and sustain me. Help me to be more like Jesus Christ, the tree planted by the stream of Your Holy Spirit. Amen.*

Grazia Patt Yonan is the author of numerous articles, poems, and cover stories. A public speaker and soprano soloist, she enjoys hiking, camping, playing softball and tennis, and making her own greeting cards. Grazia and her husband, Mike, have three children and make their home in Fremont, California.

# *Music for My Soul*

**Pauline Youd**

*Why are you downcast, O my soul?*
*Why so disturbed within me? Put*
*your hope in God, for I will yet praise*
*him, my Savior and my God.*
Psalm 42:11, *NIV*

This afternoon I went to a concert of American music. The words to the songs that were sung were mostly of despair, the death of hope, the agitation of a tortured concience. By intermission I said to my son, "Surely, the Lord is coming soon!" I felt empty and forlorn. I was engulfed in a gray, gloomy depression.

At one time, my life had been devoted to music. I had studied hard and practiced long hours. Drawn to the dramatic, the tragic, the mournful, I had taken pride in being able to sing difficult music, to hold my melody line despite the dissonance in the accompaniment.

But then I met Jesus, and He literally gave me a new song. Now I had a choice for the focus of my singing. I discovered the freedom of wholesome comedy, the sensitivity of comfort, the ecstasy of praise and realized I could have a different kind of impact on an audience. So I gave God my ambition. Oh, yes, once in a while I retreated to my melancholy song just to make sure that that wasn't where I wanted to be, but for the most part my music took a new, positive path.

It seems like a long time now since I made that choice. My songs of hope, love, peace, and joy have become a firmly entrenched habit. No wonder the concert was such a shock to me.

I do believe that once in a while the Lord allows us to see where we've been, what the world is like without Him, and how we might feel had we stayed with our own "Plan A."

*Dear Father, thank You for the gift of music to brighten and refresh my days. Help me to use this as one more area in my life that can bring You honor. Amen.*

Pauline Youd is a published book author. She is a former music director having worked with children's choirs and light opera. Pauline and her husband, William, have three children and make their home in Modesto, California.

# *From the Rising of the Sun*

**Callie B. Young**

*From the rising of the sun to its going
down the Lord's name is to be
praised.* Psalm 113:3, *NKJV*

A warm pinkish glow became a
scarlet ball that paled as it slowly climbed the
eastern sky. Such beauty! Such magnificence! The
early morning sunrise reminded me of the words
from Psalm 113.

A brown thrush and a robin searched for food in
the dew-wet grass while a blue jay squawked noisily
at the bird feeder. I heard other morning voices:
Billy's white hen clucking at her baby chicks; Bossy,
the brindle cow, lowing for her calf; and the pigs
squealing impatiently for their food.

Later that day when my washing machine
jammed and I had to empty it by hand, the glow of
my special day dimmed. As I shared in a shattering

experience of a family member, I felt no joy in the Lord.

Then I saw through my kitchen window two brown birds hopping on the ground under the wisteria bush. *Could there be a nest with newly-hatched baby thrushes in the bush?* My spirits lifted and a song came from my lips, "O Lord, open my lips, and my mouth shall show forth Your praise (Psalm 51:15).

As daily chores took more time and energy, thoughts of my special day faded. I was reminded again, however, of God's good gifts when the last rosy glow of the setting sun waned and an orchestra of night voices began. I heard the chirp of the crickets in the grass, a whippoorwill's call from the nearby woods, and the frogs on the meadow pond with a chorus all their own. I listened, then asked the Lord to again put a song on my lips, as I thanked Him for my day and the sights and sounds that made it special.

*Thank You, Lord, for letting me see, amid cares and problems, that You will meet my needs. From the rising of the sun to its going down, I can praise Your name. Amen.*

Callie B. Young is an author of historical books and numerous magazine articles. She enjoys working with children, flower gardening, and visiting shut-ins. Seventy-four years of age, she says, "I try to live each day to the fullest!" Callie and her husband have four grown children and reside in Pontotoc, Mississippi.

# "Come, Follow Me!"

## Beth A. Ziarnik

*My soul will rejoice in the Lord and
delight in his salvation. My whole
being will exclaim, "Who is like you,
O Lord?"* Psalm 35:9-10, *NIV*

Who is like you, O Lord? Your
beauty is in all your creation." The words welled up
in my aching heart as I sat alone outside my
campgrounds tent.

No longer would I hold the hand of a small boy
and guide him through life; my youngest son was
soon off to college. His whole senior year had been a
series of good-byes: his last high school drama, his
last forensic competition, his last musical play, his
last concert, his first and last prom. Then
graduation. Would this be our last family vacation?

A great sadness engulfed me. I knew my life was
changing and I wasn't sure I was ready. I was facing
the empty nest.

But somehow I sensed God reaching out to
comfort me in the unfolding beauty of dawn. I saw

dry weeds hugging the sandy soil like a delicate carpet of dusty rose. I saw oak trees standing tall against a blue sky, their leaves shining in the rising sun. In a flash of black and white, a red-headed woodpecker flew to a nearby tree, its busy rat-a-tat-tats echoing in the quiet of the morning. Below, a chipmunk darted across the campgrounds in bursts of quick rhythm.

Then, as I watched, I caught my breath. A small, fair-haired boy marched up the hill to the bathhouse. "I'm Jeremy!" he shouted joyously. "Follow me!"

His words hung in the air as I remembered a similar call long ago. "I'm Jesus. Come, follow Me!"

I've never regretted answering His call. Through good times and bad, I have experienced God's unfailing love. One thing will never change. I can go fearlessly into the coming years because my God will go with me.

*Lord, may I never forget that whatever changes I face in this life You are my God. I need not fear or be sad. For who is like You, O Lord? Amen.*

Beth A. Ziarnik is a published writer who enjoys reading, camping, crocheting, and cross-stitch. She and her husband, Jim, have two sons and make their home in Oshkosh, Wisconsin.

# More Inspirational Reading from Evergreen